WORLD ADVENTURE
DIVES

JACK JACKSON

NEW
HOLLAND

CONTENTS

PACIFIC OCEAN

INTRODUCTION
JACK JACKSON

In compiling this book I have chosen exhilarating and fascinating adventurous dive sites in different underwater environments across the world, that are suitable for all divers, ranging from novices accompanied by divemasters to those with considerable experience. The criteria used included quality, quantity, beauty and uniqueness of marine life, accessibility and the requirement of only a reasonable degree of physical fitness. Many of the dives listed could be carried out using Nitrox but this is not necessary. I have not chosen any sites that require technical diving using Heliox or Trimix because a very limited number of divers are trained to this level. In several instances, the area of the dive site chosen also has several other adventurous dive sites nearby, so where possible I have mentioned these. The selection offered here celebrates the diversity and excitement of the underwater world while appealing to a broad spectrum of active and armchair divers.

Adventurous divers enjoy dive sites that leave them bubbling with excitement when they leave the water; steep walls in the open sea, heart-thumping shark feeding-frenzies, the adrenaline rush of high-voltage drift dives and the atmosphere of shipwrecks. Some divers prefer clear, warm water while others are happy with limited visibility or the bounty found in cold waters.

Coral reefs usually have several distinct profiles. The top of the reef is likely to be a coral garden with smaller species of fish and crustaceans. Slopes or drop-offs have larger Gorgonias and big fish in shoals, and walls combine both of the above together with larger pelagic species, especially when over deep water. A wall is near to the vertical and may be overhanging or undercut, drop-offs are steep slopes of 60–85 degrees.

Some reefs and wrecks are well below the surface in open water. To dive on these divers must descend quickly to the lee of the reefs or wrecks to find shelter from the current before they get swept clear. However, these reefs or wrecks usually have excellent diving and larger pelagic species.

Many of the more adventurous dives involve strong currents and are performed as drift-dives, which can vary from pleasantly drifting along in a gentle current to high-voltage rushes as divers are swept along walls and gullies.

Many divers perform most of their diving in temperate waters where shipwrecks are the most popular sites, but the marine life can be just as interesting as in tropical waters. In general, the visibility and surface conditions will not be that good. By contrast, when diving in the warm, clear water of the tropics, surrounded by colourful marine life, divers are likely to be more relaxed. However, it is wise to wear thin exposure suits against creatures that sting.

Any level of diver can enjoy diving around a wreck but penetrating large wrecks is advanced diving in an enclosed overhead environment where divers cannot easily reach the surface in the event of equipment failure – one should either be properly trained, or be accompanied by an instructor. The same is true for cavern and cave diving.

Divers performing many dives over several days should take a complete day off after four days to allow the nitrogen remaining in their body tissues to completely dissipate.

Whatever type of diving you prefer, most dive training agencies will have a speciality course that will teach you how to enjoy it safely. All dives should be planned in advance but deep dives, cold water dives and diving in strong currents are physically demanding and conditions can change quickly so you should always be prepared to abort a dive for safety reasons.

Previous Cannon and timbers from a wrecked Spanish galleon, Mexico
Right The USS *Oriskany* wreck emerges from the gloom. Florida, USA

ARCTIC OCEAN

Kara Sea

Laptev Sea

Barents Sea

East Siberian Sea

NORWAY

SWEDEN
FINLAND

ESTONIA

POLAND

RUSSIAN FEDERATION

Sea of
Okhotsk

Bering
Sea

Aral
Sea

Caspian
Sea

Black Sea

GREECE
TURKEY

WRECK DIVING, MALTA

SYRIA

Mediterranean Sea
ISRAEL

Suez Canal

DOLPHIN REEF, ISRAEL

LIBYA
EGYPT

THE SS THISTLEGORM, EGYPT

WRECKS AND STRONG CURRENTS, EGYPT

NIGHT DIVING, SUDAN

SUDAN

IRAQ

IRAN

PAKISTAN

SAUDI
ARABIA

Red Sea

OMAN

YEMEN

Arabian Sea

NORTH
KOREA

SOUTH
KOREA

East
China
Sea

CHINA

Sea of
Japan

JAPAN

TAIWAN

PACIFIC OCEAN

INDIA

MYANMAR
(BURMA)

Bay of
Bengal

THAILAND

VIETNAM

PHILIPPINES

WRECK DIVING, THE PHILIPPINES

South
China
Sea

BIG FISH, THE PHILIPPINES

WHALE SHARKS, THAILAND

SRI LANKA

MANTA RAYS, MICRONESIA

WWII WRECKS, MICRONESIA

MANTA RAYS, MALDIVES

MALDIVES

BLUE CORNER AND JELLYFISH LAKE, MICRONESIA

MUCK DIVING, BORNEO

MICRONESIA

MALAYSIA

SINGAPORE

TURTLES AND PRISTINE REEFS, MALAYSIA

DEMOCRATIC
REPUBLIC OF
CONGO

KENYA

PAPUA NEW
GUINEA

MELANESIA

SEYCHELLES

TANZANIA

INDONESIA

COMOROS

INDIAN OCEAN

ANGOLA

MOZAMBIQUE

MADAGASCAR

MAURITIUS

Mozambique Channel

Timor Sea

AIRCRAFT WRECKS, PAPUA NEW GUINEA

SOLOMON
ISLANDS

Coral Sea

FIJI

VANUATU

GREAT BARRIER REEF, AUSTRALIA

NEW
CALEDONIA

WHALE SHARKS, AUSTRALIA

AUSTRALIA

SOUTH AFRICA

GREAT WHITE SHARKS, SOUTH AFRICA

Great
Australian
Bight

CAVE DIVING, NEW ZEALAND

SARDINE AND SQUID RUNS, SOUTH AFRICA

NEW
ZEALAND

Tasman
Sea

ANTARCTIC (SOUTHERN) OCEAN

ANTARCTICA

ECOLOGICAL DIVING

The growing awareness of environmental issues has given rise to ecotourism – managing tourism in an ecologically sustainable way. The capital investment necessary to develop ecotourism is minimal, employment becomes available for the local population and long term profits exceed those of logging or overfishing.

Many divers, dive operators and diving resorts lead the field in protecting marine ecosystems. However, as reefs attract increasing numbers of tourists and further resorts, greater controls become necessary to prevent the reefs from being damaged.

Environmentalists can go too far. If rules in one area are too strict, operators give up as divers and snorkellers go elsewhere. Without divers around to keep an eye on the animals and the coral reef, there is more chance of fishermen using destructive methods.

Many people are also concerned about the damage done unwittingly by divers. Keeping the popular areas of the marine environment ecologically sustainable depends as much on divers as it does on the dive operators and resorts; some areas close dive sites periodically to 'rest' them.

FOR ECOLOGICAL DIVING DIVERS SHOULD:
- Master good buoyancy control; coral is killed by divers touching it while adjusting their buoyancy.
- Be properly weighted and have all equipment tucked in to avoid touching any marine organisms.
- If you must settle on the seabed to practise diving exercises or adjust equipment, do so in a sandy area away from coral.
- If you are about to collide with a coral stabilize yourself with your fingertips on a part of the reef that is already dead.
- Do not use deep fin-strokes next to the reef – the surge of water stresses delicate organisms.
- Except on wrecks, do not wear gloves in warm waters, this will avoid the temptation to hold onto live corals.
- Only use reef hooks where absolutely necessary and then on a dead part of the reef.
- Do not move marine organisms around to photograph them or hitch rides on turtles, manta rays or whale sharks, it causes them considerable stress.
- Avoid several people crowding into underwater caverns and caves at the same time and do not stay in them for too long as divers' exhausted air is trapped under the roof of the cave and creatures living there suffocate.
- Do not participate in spear-fishing for sport – selective killing of the larger fish upsets the reproductive chain.
- At night, strong lights dazzle and confuse fish.

- Do not collect or purchase marine souvenirs.
- Before booking a dive trip with an operator, ask about the company's environmental policy. Avoid boats that cause unnecessary anchor damage, have bad oil leaks, or discharge untreated sewage near to reefs.
- Some operations will allow clients to offset the carbon emissions of their flights.
- Some resorts have alternative ways of generating some or all of their electricity without using fossil fuels.
- Some resorts insist on clients using environmentally safe biodegradable soap.
- Some resorts conserve water by less frequent washing of towels and sheets, have reduced-flow fixtures in bathrooms and direct grey (used) water to less important uses such as watering lawns and gardens.

- Some resorts collect rainwater and have systems for biological decomposition of solid organic materials into a product that can be used to enrich garden soils (composting). This enrichment not only nourishes the soil but also helps increase moisture retention and thus decrease the need for additional watering.
- Some regions operate as a marine park, charging for entry and use the fees to protect the environment and its marine inhabitants.
- Most operators get involved in local clean-up gatherings.
- Some operators use paying tourist-divers to help scientists with surveys of the local species.
- On any excursion, whether with an operator or privately organized, make sure that any rubbish is disposed of properly on land.

Below A diver cruises over the coral at Cod Hole, Australia

Overpage A great barracuda drifts under the crow's nest of the USCG *Duane* wreck, Florida, USA

WRECK DIVING
EAST COAST USA AND BERMUDA

The east coast of America is one of the most active SCUBA diving areas in the world. Washed by the warm waters of the Gulf Stream, there is an amazing collection of shipwrecks, from Spanish galleons to vessels sunk specifically as artificial reefs.

The Florida Keys combine coral reefs, marine sanctuaries and wrecks that attract both novice divers and experienced wreck divers. The United States Coastguard cutters *Bibb* and *Duane* were sunk as artificial reefs just south of Molasses Reef in November 1987. The huge landing ship dock USS *Spiegel Grove* joined the *Bibb* and *Duane* some years later, and in the Gulf of Mexico the USS *Oriskany* became the world's largest artificial reef in 2006.

Bermuda, a British overseas territory 1,437 km (893 miles) east of Charleston, South Carolina, is also in the path of the Gulf Stream and has the northernmost coral reef system in the world. Its treacherous reefs have resulted in over 350 documented wrecks. Often dubbed the 'Shipwreck Capital of the Atlantic', treasure hunters found several wrecks with cargoes that included gold and jewellery and thus the name, 'Bermuda's Golden Circle' was coined.

The southern part of the east coast of America, and together with Bermuda are suffering from an invasion of Indo-Pacific lionfish, which have no natural predators in this area.

THE GRAVEYARD OF THE ATLANTIC
SS *PROTEUS*

One of the most popular wrecks in this area is the SS *Proteus*, a 4,836 ton, 124 m (406 ft)-long, 14.6 m (48 ft)-beam steamship sunk in a collision with the SS *Cushing*, 40 km (25 miles) south of Hatteras Inlet on August 19th 1918. Today she lies in 38 m (125 ft) of water, listing to port and rising 9 m (30 ft) from the bottom. The wreck is mostly intact so it is easy for divers to find their way around. The steering mechanism is unbroken, there are three main boilers, the propeller, and a spare propeller. The marine life includes stingrays and cobia and shoals of spotted raggedtooth (sandtiger or grey nurse) sharks that gather in October/November.

Right Goliath grouper inside a wreck off Key West, Florida
Overpage Divers inside the USS *Oriskany* wreck

WRECKS AND THE LAW

Most countries have different and often confusing laws regarding diving on wrecks. Many Third World governments have none at all, and others, despite giving permission for salvage, often renege on agreements and confiscate anything valuable found.

There are problems over ownership, archaeological and heritage value and loss of life; the loss of life issue is further complicated by often only covering the sanctity of military personnel in designated 'war graves' and not civilian casualties either in wartime or peacetime. Governments cannot control war graves that are not in their own waters and often governments contradict themselves by issuing licences for salvors to salvage valuables from a war grave but not allowing others to dive on it.

Where voluntary restraints exist divers should obey them to avoid giving bureaucrats the excuse to ban all sport diving on wrecks. Those diving wrecks in their own country should first become thoroughly conversant with the local laws before diving in foreign countries. Local dive operators should understand local regulations.

ATLANTIC AND MEDITERRANEAN

Above A goliath grouper hangs above a shrimp boat wreck off the Florida coast

FLORIDA – USS *ORISKANY*

The aircraft carrier USS *Oriskany* became the world's largest artificial reef when it was sunk on May 17th 2006, 42 km (22.5 miles) southeast of Pensacola Pass in the Gulf of Mexico. The bottom of the ship is 65 m (212 ft)-deep but the island is now only 24 m (80 ft) below the surface and easily accessible to the average diver.

The USS *Oriskany* was laid down on 1st May 1944 and launched on 13th October 1945. Construction was suspended on 12th August 1947 and the vessel redesigned and updated, which changed her dimensions. She was commissioned on 25th September 1950. An Essex-class aircraft carrier with a displacement of 27,100 tons she was 278 m (911 ft)-long, 45 m (147 ft)-beam and 9.3 m (30.5 ft)-draft and was nicknamed the 'Mighty O'. She served in Korea and Vietnam and was decommissioned in September 1976.

When sunk, the ship was upright with the bow facing south, the flight deck at 40 m (130 ft). However, 12 m (40 ft)-seas from Hurricane Gustav in 2008 gave her a slight starboard list and helped her sink further into the sand by as much as 2.5-3 m (8-10 ft).

The stairways and railings of the Oriskany are already covered with marine life. The fish include damsels, triggerfish, filefish, sharks, amberjacks and passing barracuda. Because of the depth, the lower structures are only suitable for technical divers.

BERMUDA – SS *CRISTÓBAL COLÓN*

One of the largest wrecks in Bermudian waters, the SS *Cristóbal Colón* is a 150 m (492 ft)-long Spanish luxury liner launched in 1923. She was heading for Mexico to load arms for the Spanish Civil War when she ran aground north of Bermuda on October 25th 1936. She was easily looted and salvaged, and during World War II US Navy aircraft pilots used her for bombing practice. Broken in two and divided by the reef, the *Cristóbal Colón*'s wreckage stretches over a large area, ranging in depth from 5 m (16 ft) at the bow to 25 m (82 ft) at the semi-intact stern. A huge wreck that takes several dives to cover, like most of Bermuda's wrecks she is relatively shallow and the marine life is prolific. Propellers, turbines, boilers and unexploded artillery shells litter the ocean floor.

FACTS

CLIMATE

North Carolina is located in a warm temperate zone where it is seasonal but moderate, January averages 7°C (45°F) and August can reach 36°C (97°F).

Caribbean-like, Florida is sub-tropical with temperatures from 18-23°C (65-73°F) in winter and up to 30°C (86°F) in late summer, most rainfall is concentrated between May and October and at sea the wind gives a cooling breeze. The hurricane season formally begins on June 1st and ends on November 30th but historically, the chances of hurricane activity are greater between August 15th and October 1st.

Bermuda is sub-tropical with temperatures from 18-23°C (65-73°F) in winter and up to 30°C (86°F) in late summer. The hurricane season is June to November but most hurricanes occur from August to October.

SEASONALITY

All wrecks in the north are best dived in the northern summer but remember this is the North Atlantic, so it can get really rough.

Florida: Year round but the hurricane season can be a problem.

Bermuda: Best if dived in the northern summer but the hurricane season is a problem. Bermuda can be dived all year round and has wrecks all around the islands so there will be leeward diving somewhere in most weathers.

GETTING THERE

North Carolina wreck sites are similarly reached from various towns and cities including Morehead City, Beaufort, Wilmington and Hatteras.

Florida: Flights to Miami.

Bermuda: Fly to L.F. Wade International Airport on St David's Island.

WATER TEMPERATURE

Off North Carolina the range is from 13°C (55°F) in winter and spring, rising to 26°C (80°F) in late summer.

Florida: Ranges from 22°C (72°F) from December to March and up to 29°C (84°F) from April to November.

Bermuda: Ranges from 20°C (68°F) in January to 27°C (80°F) in August.

QUALITY OF MARINE LIFE

North Carolina has a mixture of cold water species and tropical species that have arrived on the Gulf Stream. Florida and Bermuda have a rich collection of tropical species.

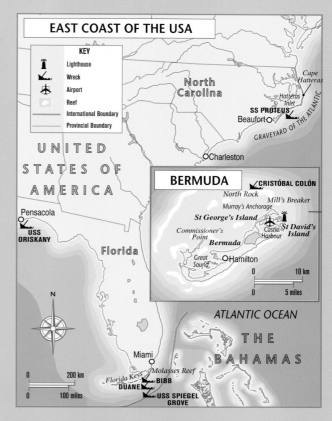

DEPTH OF DIVES

Most of the popular North Carolina wrecks are in the 24-46 m (79-151 ft)-range.

Florida: From the surface to beyond the accepted limits for recreational diving on air.

Bermuda: Most wrecks are shallow, generally less than 30 m (98 ft).

SAFETY

North Carolina's other wrecks can be enjoyed by most divers though the deeper ones require more training.

Florida: The majority of dives can be enjoyed by most divers but the deeper parts of the USS *Oriskany* require more training or technical diving.

Bermuda: Generally easy and safe diving.

WRECK DIVING
SCAPA FLOW, SCOTLAND

Scapa Flow is one of the world's largest natural anchorages and has been used as shelter by ships for several centuries.

Located in the Orkney Islands, which lie off the northern tip of Scotland 24 km (15 miles)-north of the mainland, Scapa Flow is approximately 24 km (15 miles) from north to south, 13 km (8 miles)-wide and 363 sq km (140 sq miles) in area. Scapa Flow was an important northern base for the British fleets in both world wars. In World War I, the remnants of the German fleet were scuttled there. In World War II, Scapa Flow was heavily defended with anti-aircraft batteries, minefields and further blockships. However in the early hours of 14th October 1939, the German submarine *U-47* commanded by Lieutenant Günther Prien managed to pass between the main island of Orkney and Lamb Holm into Scapa Flow. The submarine passed between two northerly block-ships and torpedoed the old Revenge Class battleship HMS *Royal Oak*. The *U-47*'s second torpedo attack blew a 9 m (30 ft) hole in *Royal Oak* and as a result she quickly flooded and capsized. Of the 1,400 crew, 833 were lost. The wreck is now a protected war grave and each year there are memorial services on the anniversary of the sinking.

Three days after this submarine attack, four Luftwaffe Junkers Ju 88 bombers raided Scapa Flow in one of the first aerial attacks on Britain during the war. The attack badly damaged the elderly base ship, the Super Dreadnought Class Battleship HMS *Iron Duke*, but she was refloated and saw continued service until the conclusion of hostilities. One bomber was shot down by an anti-aircraft battery on Hoy.

There are many superb wrecks for diving in Scapa Flow but everyone wants to dive on the German fleet. Most of these have been salvaged but the remaining warships are the main attraction. Many divers believe that you can only dive the German fleet using Nitrox or Trimix, and that all dives should be treated as decompression dives. In fact diving in Scapa Flow can be as simple or as complicated as divers want to make it. There are dives that are quite shallow and suitable for novices. Where areas are tidal they must be dived at slack water.

Scapa Flow has the best wreck diving in Europe. Most of what remains of the German fleet is breaking up and is dangerous; many divers think that the blockships *Doyle, Gobernador Bories* and the *Tabarka* at the entrance to Burra Sound are the most interesting. There are also three designated War Graves where no diving is allowed without permission from the Admiralty: HMS *Hampshire*, HMS *Vanguard* and HMS *Royal Oak*.

Right A diver investigating marine life on the blockship SS *Doyle*

RESTRICTIONS ON DIVING ON MARITIME WAR GRAVES

A small minority of divers cannot resist disturbing wrecks and the temptation of removing brass and other artefacts. Diving on deep wrecks has been facilitated by the introduction of technical diving for recreational divers and this has worried relatives of those who lost their lives in maritime conflicts and disasters. In an effort to give greater protection to maritime war graves and military wrecks against trophy hunting, some wrecks owned by governments have been designated as 'Controlled Sites' - where no diving is allowed without a special permit.

Below The deck cleat of SMS *Karlsruhe II*

SS DOYLE

Lying across the current between 13 and 17 m (43 and 56 ft) on the inside of Burra Sound, the *Doyle* was a single-screw coastal vessel built in Troon, Ayrshire. 1,671 tons and 79 m (260 ft)-long she was requisitioned by the Admiralty and sunk as a blockship on 7th October 1914. In those days those in charge of such scuttling did not make enough allowance for changes in tides and the vessel drifted deeper into Burra Sound and ended up directly across the tidal race where she lies today.

Despite not being one of the German fleet, the *Doyle* is one of the more satisfying dives at Scapa Flow because of the shallow depth, good visibility and prodigious invertebrate life, due to the strong tides, which also clear the wreck of silt.

Lying on her port side, the *Doyle* is very open allowing divers to penetrate at various levels. The propeller is still in place. The more exposed hull is covered in dwarf plumose anemones, ballan and cuckoo wrasse, conger eels, shoals of juvenile saithe and pollock and lobsters are encountered.

SMS *KARLSRUHE II*

Lying between 14 and 27 m (46 and 89 ft), northwest of the northwest tip of Cava, the Königsberg Light Cruiser *Karlsruhe II* is deteriorating badly but is a popular dive as it is the shallowest of the High Seas Fleet and therefore has the best ambient light and allows the longest bottom time. Built by Kaiserliche Werft of Wilhelmshaven, the vessel displaced 5,440 tons and was 151 m (495 ft)-long and 14.2 m (47 ft)-beam.

Well broken up and partly salvaged though now registered as a memorial monument and protected from further salvage efforts, the *Karlsruhe* lies listing on her starboard side with her bow guns collapsed from the deck and settled into the silt. Much of the deck is torn open. The starboard deck comes as shallow as 15 m (49 ft) and the seabed at the stern is only 28 m (92 ft). The wreck is easy to navigate around, can be penetrated at the larger holes and has lots of marine life including wrasse, cod, pollock, plumose anemones, brittle stars, starfish, sponges, crabs, shrimps, nudibranchs and sea urchins. There can be a strong current.

FACTS

CLIMATE
Usually wet and windy, air temperatures can reach 28°C (82°F) in summer.

SEASONALITY
If the weather is good enough the wrecks can be dived all year round, but in most cases should only be dived at slack water. The water is warmer from August to October.

GETTING THERE
There is a car ferry daily from Scrabster on the Scottish mainland to Stromness to connect with Scapa Flow charter vessels. Flights are available to nearby Kirkwall from Aberdeen, Edinburgh and Glasgow.

WATER TEMPERATURE
Water temperatures can range from 14°C (57°F) in August and September down to as low as 5°C (41°F) in January and February.

QUALITY OF MARINE LIFE
Very good, colder water always has plenty of species of fish and invertebrates.

KEY
10 Road
Wreck
Dive Site

Mainland · A964 · Graemsay · DOYLE · Linksness · GOBERNADOR BORIES · Burra Sound · SCAPA FLOW · HMS ROYAL OAK · Barrel of Butter · KARLSRUHE II · B9047 · Hoy · Cava · SCAPA FLOW · Skerry Sound · Rysa Little · N · HMS VANGUARD · Calf of Flotta · Burray · Fara · Flotta · Water Sound · Lyness · 0 4 km · 0 2 miles

DEPTH OF DIVES
From 3-15 m (10-49 ft) on the blockships to the east; 12-18 m (39-59 ft) on the blockships to the west and from 15-42 m (49-138 ft) on the Light Cruisers and Battleships.

SAFETY
Conditions can be difficult and require a minimum of advanced open water with some wreck skills but many novice divers are fine if accompanied by an instructor. In midsummer there can be large stinging jellyfish and currents are strong and can be fierce.

GREAT WHITE SHARKS
SOUTH AFRICA

When they are not actually on migration, the largest great white shark population in the world is thought to be off the coast of South Africa, with the highest concentrations along the southwest and south coasts of the Western Cape.

The great white shark, *Carcharodon carcharias*, also known as white pointer, white shark, or white death, reaches a length of more than 6 m (20 ft) and weighs up to 2,250 kg (4,960 lb). The great white shark is the world's largest known predatory fish.

Cage diving with great white sharks in South Africa began at Dyer Island near Gansbaai in 1991 but when it became popular and more operators joined the mêlée, operators looked for alternative sites; two operators moved to Seal Island in False Bay near Simon's Town and one operator to Mossel Bay, half way between Cape Town and Port Elizabeth, approximately 392 km (244 miles) east of Cape Town. The water tends to be slightly warmer at Mossel Bay.

Dyer Island off Gansbaai is still the main area for most commercial operators but Seal Island in False Bay also has breaching behaviour, is only 35-minutes from Cape Town and is not open to the large seas that pound Dyer Island during the best time to see the sharks – the winter months of mid-April to mid-September. June, July and August are the best months for encountering the animals.

Seal Island in False Bay has a colony of some 64,000 cape fur seals and great white sharks often leap clear of the water (breaching) by as much as 3 m (10 ft) when hunting them. The operators here specialize in viewing natural behaviour so the amount of chumming is minimal. This area does require divers to have basic scuba certification.

Charter boats to Seal Island depart from the old port of Simon's Town and the great white sharks here are often larger than those seen elsewhere off South Africa.

Charter boats operating at Gansbaai, 160 km (99 miles), two-hours drive east of Cape Town, depart from the harbour of Kleinbaai and head for Dyer Island some 10 km (5.2 miles), 20-minutes offshore. Dyer Island is a nature reserve and includes the surrounding water 500 m (1640 ft) out to sea; boats may only enter this area with a permit from the Department of Nature Conservation and the number of boats in the channel is limited at any one time to prevent overcrowding. A warden stationed on Dyer Island protects the birds that breed there.

Between Dyer Island and Geyser Rock there is a channel known as Shark Alley where the boats can anchor in about 5 m (16 ft) of water and chum with mashed fish and fish oil. The coxswain rounds Dyer Island and approaches Shark Alley from the seaward side so as to avoid the large breakers that often occur in the landward entrance. Shark Alley is roughly 350 m (1,148 ft)-long, 250 m (820 ft)-wide and 5 to 10 m (16-33 ft)-deep.

Geyser Rock is so called because the action of the waves breaking on the rock sends water high into the sky like a natural geyser. It has a colony of some 50,000 cape fur seals that attract the great white sharks. It seems that the great white sharks are not really interested in feeding on the young pups but prefer to wait until they mature into more blubbery sub-adults. The operators here focus purely on divers who want to observe great white sharks underwater or non-divers who wish to see them from the surface. This is the main place to go for those who wish to see the animals close up.

Right A diver alongside a great white shark, Dyer Island
Overpage A great white shark breaks the surface at Shark Alley

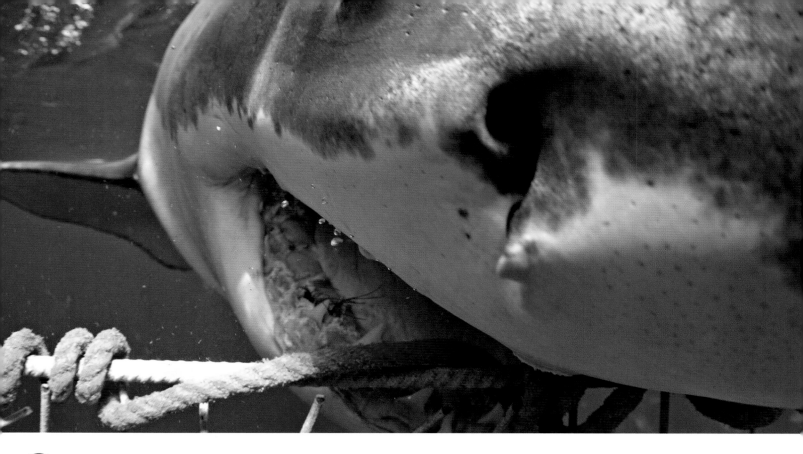

Above A great white mouths a diver's cage, Seal Island

ATLANTIC AND MEDITERRANEAN

THE ETHICS OF FEEDING

Conservationists argue that feeding fish alters their natural feeding behaviour, affects their health, makes them dependent on divers and could attract more dangerous predators. They have a point with regard to feeding humphead (Napoleon) wrasse with eggs or any fish with food that is not part of its natural diet, but others argue that feeding does not alter long-term behaviour. Most animals are opportunistic feeders, not averse to carrion and the amount of food that divers introduce is minimal so the fish do not become reliant on it. At the Cayman Island's Stingray City, the rays are fed many times each day, yet are still observed feeding naturally and at shark feeds elsewhere a few dominant animals take most of the food while most sharks go without. More importantly, the quantity of divers that these themed events attract causes governments to realize that the animals are worth more when kept alive for tourism than wiped out by fishermen. It is estimated that half of the diving/snorkelling dollars spent in Grand Cayman are on the stingray feeds and that in the Bahamas, shark-feeds bring in over $60 million in a year.

Things must be kept in perspective. Shark attacks have occurred in areas where no feeding occurs and there has not been any obvious reason for these attacks. I have been bitten by both large groupers and sharks although no feeding had previously occurred at the dive sites concerned.

Even where hundreds of non-cage shark-feeds are performed yearly with hand-feeding and/or large amounts of bait, there have been very few injuries and those that do occur were mostly to those performing the hand-feeding. The incident-rate is well within the range of adventure sports in general and considerably safer than mountaineering, skiing or snowboarding – many more people are killed by bee-stings or lightning.

If done in a responsible manner, shark-feeding dives are reasonably safe. As divers we are privileged to have remarkably close encounters with wildlife underwater, often within arm's length. Feeding fish is an emotive issue – you will have to make up your own mind.

All licensed great white shark cage operators in South Africa now operate according to strict government regulations and a code of conduct. The method of chumming as well as the bait used is also prescribed by the authorities. Only natural foodstuffs may be used and anything foreign to the diet of the sharks is strictly forbidden. Only natural fibre ropes may be used to attach the bait to the boat, not nylon.

The operators all work in a similar fashion. Once the boat has reached a position where the sharks are regularly encountered, chum and some larger fish bait is placed into the water and the smell of the chum carries down-current. Everybody then waits for the great white sharks to find the chum, which can take anything from minutes to several hours. Once the sharks are around the boat, a shark cage that floats at the surface is lowered into the water. Divers then enter the cage through the top and wait for the shark to approach closer. Divers are never more than one metre below the surface. Once in the diving cage, divers usually breathe through a 'hookah system' where air is supplied from a compressor through a long hose to each diver. In some cases the tourists either snorkel or just take a breath and hold it. As the cage is battered around on the surface, some visitors may require anti-seasickness medications.

When the first shark appears, baited lines are drawn in towards the boat so that the shark is drawn in closer. It must be remembered that these are wild animals so no guarantees can be given that they will be sighted on any one particular day. It is therefore advisable to budget for at least two consecutive days of diving.

Bracing against the sides of the cage the divers point their wide-angle lenses towards the action as usually there is not enough time to compose through viewfinders. The divers soon run out of film, memory card or video, but the action is always too enthralling to miss. Divers tend to remain in the cages until they either run out of air or become too cold, then climb out to let others take their place.

In 1991 South Africa was the first country in the world to give great white sharks protection, since then it has been illegal to hunt or deal in any part of the sharks.

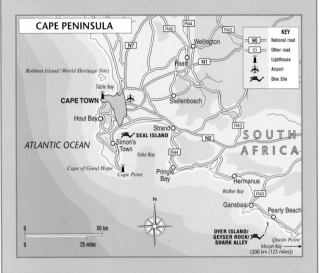

FACTS

CLIMATE
Mediterranean climate with winter rainfall. Summer is November to February and winter from May to July.

SEASONALITY
Mid-April to September/October.

GETTING THERE
International flights to Johannesburg then connect to Cape Town.

WATER TEMPERATURE
12-19°C (54-66°F).

QUALITY OF MARINE LIFE
Very good for great white sharks.

DEPTH OF DIVES
The surface to 1 m (3.3 ft).

SAFETY
The cage and on the boat at anchor tend to produce more seasickness than a boat underway.

WRECK DIVING
MALTA

The Republic of Malta is a small archipelago in the middle of the Mediterranean Sea, 93 km (58 miles) south of Sicily (Italy) and 288 km (179 miles) north of Africa.

These strategically-located islands have been ruled and fought over by various powers over the centuries. Made up of three main islands, the total area is 316 sq km (122 sq miles). Gozo is 67 sq km (26 sq miles), Comino 3 sq km (1 sq mile) and Malta is 246 sq km (95 sq miles). These rugged islands are mostly made up of an ancient limestone reef. Malta has no rivers or lakes and very few trees, which helps to ensure the good visibility.

Malta has long been a favourite family holiday destination for tourists from all over Europe. It used to be even more popular before the northern Red Sea became particularly cheap and easy to get to but Malta is fighting back with several wrecks purposely sunk as artificial reefs.

Malta is a year-round diving destination, with the water temperature dropping no lower than 14°C (57°F) in winter and reaching 26°C (80°F) in late summer. Diving in Malta is easy, at most sites you can drive almost to the water's edge, kit up and jump in. The bottom shelves down in steps to reach 25-30 m (82-98 ft) within a 5-minute swim, so there is a choice of diving depths to suit all levels of ability. The rock has been eroded to produce caves, caverns, overhangs and swim-throughs. There are almost no tides but sometimes there are underwater currents that flow in the opposite direction to the wind and the surface sea conditions.

The visibility is good but there are not any large marine animals. There are few colourful fish or pelagics.

The marine life divers are most likely to encounter includes barracuda, groupers, amberjack, bream, wrasse, damselfish, octopuses, squid, cuttlefish, scorpionfish, flying fish, flying gurnard, stingrays, the occasional moray eel and sea horses.

Due to the islands' position during World War II, there are many wrecks dating from that conflict. These wrecks are all well documented, including those of several aircraft, but there are also deeper wrecks that can be visited using mixed gas technical diving.

MV *IMPERIAL EAGLE*

The MV *Imperial Eagle* was launched in 1938 as the *New Royal Lady*. She was requisitioned by the Royal Navy in 1940 for transport duties and in 1944 was attached to the US Navy. In 1957 she moved to Malta, and in 1958 was renamed MV *Imperial Eagle* and turned into a passenger ferry that operated between Gozo and Malta until 1968.

45m (148ft)-long, with a beam of 9m (30ft), the MV *Imperial Eagle* was sold to the local Diving community on 28th November 1995 to be sunk as an artificial reef for divers off Qawra point and to form the main attraction for an Underwater Marine Park Project. She was scuttled on the 19th July 1999 in 42 m (138 ft) of water, 300 m (984 ft) northeast of Qawra Point.

The wreck of the MV *Imperial Eagle* now lies upright on sand between Qawra Point and Qrejten Point, the average depth is 28 m (92 ft) and the maximum depth 42 m (138 ft).

Nowadays this site is regarded as a deep dive in an undersea valley if using air. The first stop is the 3 m (10 ft), 13 ton (13.2 tonne) glass reinforced fibre covered concrete statue of Christ (*see over*). Divers then proceed to the bows of the ship. Intact and relatively new, her

Right The Statue of Christ (Kristu L-Bahhar)

radial spoke steering wheel is quite photogenic. She has a fine covering of algae and sponges and is home to many wrasse, chromis, bogue and grouper. This is a boat dive on an exposed site so it can be choppy with some current.

THE STATUE OF CHRIST (KRISTU L-BAHHAR)

The 13-ton statue of Christ is made of concrete and covered with glass reinforced fibre; it was designed by the sculptor Alfred Camilleri Cauchi. Commissioned by a committee of divers led by Mr. Raniero Borg, it commemorates Pope John Paul II's visit to Malta in 1990. After being blessed by the Pope it was lowered onto the seabed at 18 m (59 ft) close to St. Paul's Islands. At that time the water there was very clear and the statue could be seen from the surface but the visibility soon turned so bad that this was no longer possible. Ten years later it was lifted out of the water and taken to a conservation area next to the MV *Imperial Eagle* off Qawra Point where more divers were likely to see it.

Below The propeller of a Bristol Beaufighter aircraft wrecked off Malta

FACTS

CLIMATE

Mediterranean climate with seasonal winds and occasional heavy rain. Temperatures vary from 11°C (52°F) in winter to 35°C (95°F) in summer.

SEASONALITY

Malta is a year round diving destination and while there can be periodic winter storms, there is always a lee shore and divers are still able to dive on any number of wrecks. The best conditions are from May to the end of September.

GETTING THERE

There are direct flights to Luqa Airport on Malta from all over Europe and much of the Middle East. In summer there are charter flights from several provincial airports. There is a helicopter service between Malta & Gozo, but most people drive north to the ferry terminal at Cirkewwa and cross by ferry to Mgarr harbour on Gozo. The journey time is around 25 minutes.

WATER TEMPERATURE

14°C (57°F) in winter, 26°C (80°F) in summer.

QUALITY OF MARINE LIFE

Very good for invertebrates and sea horses but there are very few large shoals of fish.

DEPTH OF DIVES

25 m (82 ft) to deeper than recreational divers should go on air, so be careful of your depth.

SAFETY

Local fishermen are sometimes resentful of divers when shore diving as they maintain that divers scare away the fish!

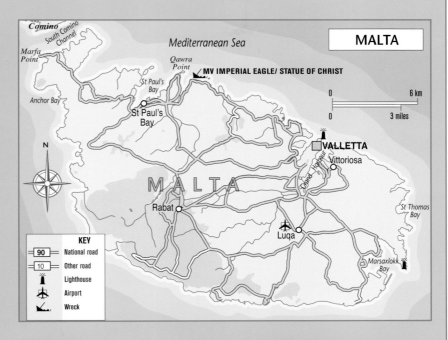

THE ISLANDS

The second-largest island, Gozo, also called Ghawdex, is 25-minutes by ferry from the larger island of Malta and has 43 km (27 miles) of coastline. This island is the most popular with visiting divers. The smallest of the inhabited islands is Comino, also called Kemmuna. The largest island is Malta, which has a coastline of 136 km (85 miles). The longest distance on the island is 27 km (17 miles) from the northwest to the southeast. In addition there are four uninhabited islands: Cominotto, St. Paul's, Fungus Rock and Fifla.

Although many of the islands' dive operators offer boat dives, most diving is done from the shore, to some of the top wreck and reef sites.

The Special Needs Assessment Study for Gozo identified the need to develop niche tourism markets such as scuba diving for Gozo's tourism development. Financed by the Malta Tourist Authority and the European Union (EU) Niche Tourism Project for the Island of Gozo, more purposely sunk wrecks, the vessels MV *Comino Land* and MV *Karwela*, were scuttled just off the Gozo coast at Ix-Xatt I-Ahmar, on Saturday 12th August 2006 and an extra recompression chamber has been added in Gozo General Hospital.

CAVERN DIVING
MENORCA

The island of Menorca (also known as Minorca) is the least commercial, easternmost and second largest of Spain's Balearic Islands, which comprise Mallorca, (Majorca), Menorca, Ibiza and Formentera.

Located in the Mediterranean Sea, east-northeast of Mallorca and approximately 230 km (143 miles) south of Barcelona on the Spanish mainland, the island is roughly 47 km (29 miles)-long and up to 19 km (12 miles)-wide. It has an area of 668 sq km (258 sq miles) and 216 km (134 miles) of coastline. Slightly further north than the other Balearic Islands, it is usually a few degrees cooler, which can be a definite advantage in the summer.

For divers, as well as having clear water and good marine life, Menorca is known for having a variety of underwater caverns in its limestone. Some of these are tunnels with dead ends while others are large chambers with shafts branching off. Some of the caverns are good sites for teaching divers the correct way to approach real cave diving in enclosed overhead environments: the rule of thirds on breathing gasses, backup equipment, careful light finning and laying a safety guideline so that the divers can find their way back to safety by running the line through their fingers in zero visibility.

PONT D'EN GIL CAVERN

The famous Pont d'en Gil cavern system is situated on the west coast at Sa Cigonya near the old Moorish capital Ciutadella. The entrance to the cave system is via a large cave mouth through which you emerge into a cavern decorated with stalagmites and stalactites. Suitable for all standards of divers it is considered the best dive in the Western Mediterranean Sea. It is a world-class cavern that stretches 220 m (722 ft) inland. The dive is shallow and divers can spend most of their time along the surface inside the cave, thus using very little air.

Located next to an arm of land that surrounds a sheltered cove called Caleta de Sa Cigonya, the dive boat anchors here and this is the deepest part of the dive at 12 m (39 ft). From here on the cavern gradually gets shallower until divers eventually surface in the cave to look at the rock formations.

There are two entrances, the main entrance, some 20 m (66 ft)-wide and 18 m (59 ft)-high where fallen rocks from the roof litter the seafloor, and another where divers swim through a constricted section. A layer of freshwater lies on top of the seawater throughout the cavern and there are few places where daylight cannot be seen. Divers going further into the cavern will find stalagmites and stalactites both below and above water. Some stalagmites at the seabed are broken while others join stalactites descending from the roof to form columns.

After a short swim the divers surface inside in a huge cavern full of air with its roof some 200 m (656 ft)-high. The water is about 6 m (20 ft)-deep and has white seabream, damselfish, moray eels, groupers, lobsters, rays, scorpionfish, shrimps and nudibranchs.

Once inside the cavern the divers observe the wonderous stalactites hanging from the roof. At the end of the cavern there is a small beach.

Stalactites and stalagmites can only form when freshwater drips from the roof of an otherwise dry limestone cave. Each drip leaves tiny traces of previously dissolved limestone on the ceiling, then another tiny amount as it strikes the floor. Over thousands of years, the deposited limestone builds up, first as tiny straws, then as larger columns. When sea levels were lower

Right A diver enters the Pont D'en Gil Cavern

ATLANTIC AND MEDITERRANEAN

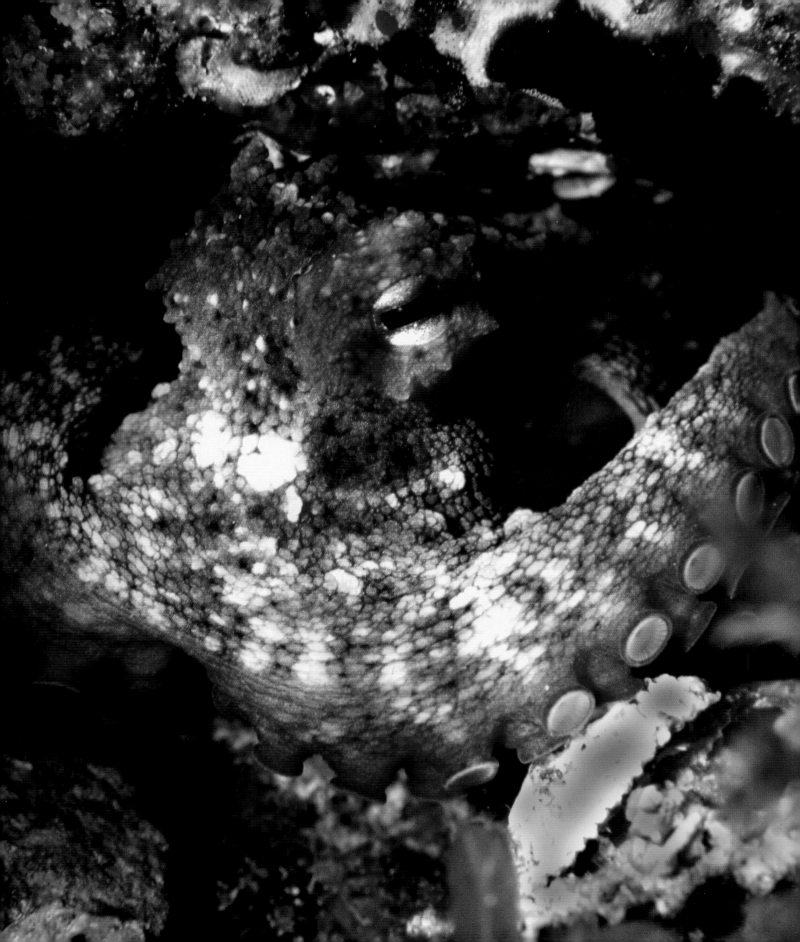

during the last ice age, stalagmites and stalactites formed in Pont d'en Gil. When the ice age ended, sea levels rose again and saltwater filled the lower parts of the cavern. The spectacular submerged cave formations were frozen in time for divers to marvel at.

Other caves/caverns regularly dived in Menorca by all standards of diver include:

TOM'S BELFRY – This site off Cap d'en Font has to be one of the most spectacular cavern dives available anywhere. Divers swim up a phreatic tube – one formed by a volcanic eruption, from which steam or mud is expelled when groundwater occurring below the water table comes into contact with hot magma or rock.

CATHEDRAL CAVERN – is the most easterly cave off Cap d'en Font and can be visited on the same dive as Tom's Belfry. The entry arch is so large that it is naturally lit with diffused light for the whole of its length. The entrance is 183 m (600 ft)-high and 12 m (40 ft)-wide.

THE CORAL GALLERIES – these are near S'algar. Located beneath a rocky islet off the north end of the Isla del Aire, which is situated off the extreme southeastern tip of Menorca. The Coral Galleries are named after the diversity of ahermatypic corals, bryozoans and sponges that colonize its walls and roofs. Occupying three levels, there are several entrances with daylight illuminating almost all of the walls and roof. Just outside is the wreck site of *La Laurette*, a French man-o-war sunk in 1883, complete with cannon and musket balls.

There are eight large caverns and several smaller ones on the Isla del Aire and one of them is **THE MOON POOL**, which is another phreatic tube. This dive is for more experienced cavern divers only.

As well as caverns there is healthy fish and invertebrate life off Menorca.

Left Common octopus hides in a cavern crevice
Overpage Caribbean reef and blacktip sharks at Shark Rodeo, the Bahamas

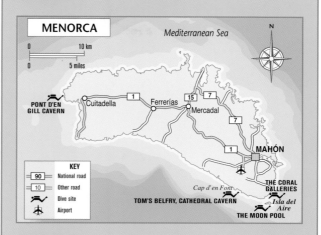

FACTS

CLIMATE
Mediterranean climate with winds, temperatures vary between 20°C in winter and 29°C in summer.

SEASONALITY
May to October. High season for non-diving tourists is July and August.

GETTING THERE
Fly to Mahon or travel by ferry from Barcelona on the Spanish mainland.

WATER TEMPERATURE
15-25°C (60-77°F)

QUALITY OF MARINE LIFE
Varied and healthy.

DEPTH OF DIVES
From the surface to 20 m (66 ft) for the caverns.

SAFETY
Divers who do not have cave-diving training should dive with an instructor.

SHARK DIVING
THE BAHAMAS

Scattered across some 181,300 sq km (70,000 sq miles) of the Atlantic Ocean, diving in the Commonwealth of the Bahamas is classified with Caribbean destinations and is the largest concentration of islands in the region.

The islands straddle the Tropic of Cancer in a northwest-southeast direction along a 1,207 km (750 mile) stretch from just off Florida in the north, to just off eastern Cuba and Haiti in the south. Roughly 644 km (400 miles)-across at their widest point, only about 40 of the 700 islands and over 2,000 islets and cays (pronounced 'keys'), are inhabited.

Most islands offer shallow reefs from 3 m (10 ft) to 15 m (49 ft) and deeper reefs at 30 m (98 ft), but many have drop-offs going deeper than sports divers should descend to. Like other destinations along the southern east coast of America, the Bahamas are suffering from an invasion of Indo-Pacific lionfish, which do not have any natural predators in the region.

In addition to world-class reefs, blue holes and wrecks, the Bahamas are famous for encounters with dolphins and shark feeds. For many years shark feeds for divers without a cage involved relatively safe sharks like Caribbean reef sharks. In recent years some operators have run trips involving larger and more unpredictable sharks such as bull, greater hammerhead and tiger sharks but a couple of these have gone tragically wrong.

The shark diving capital of the Tropical Atlantic, there are shark dives almost everywhere, some are shark-feeds but some are not and operators have perfected their own way of working.

One operator on Grand Bahama Island offers diving with tiger sharks from the safety of a cage at Tiger Beach 32 km (20 miles) off the coast of West End. This operator uses a 'hookah style' air supply system where air is supplied from a compressor through a long hose to each diver so you do not have to be a certified diver to participate. By eliminating the need for air cylinders, it is easier to move about in the cage and to take photographs. The dive boats depart for Tiger Beach from the Marina at Old Bahama Bay Resort near West End, approximately 40 km (25 miles) west of Freeport.

At Grand Bahama Island there are shark dives by different dive operators at nearby sites called Shark Alley and Shark Junction. Both sites are over a sandy-bottom at a depth of roughly 15 m (49 ft). The diving clients kneel in a semicircle while a feeder, dressed in a full, stainless steel mesh suit, hand-feeds Caribbean reef and blacktip reef sharks, groupers and snappers, which approach from all directions.

At Shark Junction, the feeder takes one fish at a time from a plastic container and feeds the sharks individually as they crowd around the scent of the bait. There are 15-20 sharks on most dives.

Between Andros and New Providence, Shark Buoy (The Deer Island Buoy or Deployed Noise and Measurement Buoy (DNM)), is out in the tongue of the ocean. Tethered in 1829 m (6,000 ft) of water it consists of a huge bottom mooring and over 1.6 km (1 mile) of polypropylene line stretching up to within 61 m (200 ft) of the surface. The last 61 m (200 ft) is steel cable that is fixed to the buoy floating on the surface. The buoy is used by the US Navy for submarine exercises. It attracts dolphinfish, wahoo, rainbow runners and small immature silky sharks, which are fed there. Dive boats tie up to the

Right A Caribbean Reef Shark cruises over a coral reef ledge
Overpage A fearsome tiger shark at West End

buoy, which is in open water so divers descend using the buoy's mooring line for reference. The Tongue of the Ocean is a deep trench that drops from around 3–5 m (10–15 ft) to 1829 m (6,000 ft). It begins off the south end of New Providence Island and runs along the eastern side of Andros, the trench is roughly 161 km (100 miles)-long.

Some of the best Bahamian shark diving is off New Providence Island, where it is the main attraction. There are four sites where divers can dive with the sharks:

either a combination of Shark Wall and Shark Arena or a combination of Shark Wall North and The Runway. At either location divers will encounter a gathering of Caribbean reef sharks. The dives take place as two dives, one without feeding such as at Shark Wall and the second with feeding such as at Shark Arena. At Shark Wall Caribbean reef and other sharks patrol the reef in anticipation of obtaining food but no food is supplied until the second dive.

Shark Arena area is a sandy seabed at 14 m (45 ft).

The shark-feeder is dressed in a chainmail suit to hand-feed Caribbean reef sharks. Some operators shark-feeders place the bait on a short barbless spear, which gives them more control over where they position the shark for clients' photography. The divers find themselves close to the sharks but so long as they keep their hands close to their bodies and remain calm the sharks are more interested in the bait.

Below Caribbean reef sharks and yellowtail snappers, West End

FACTS

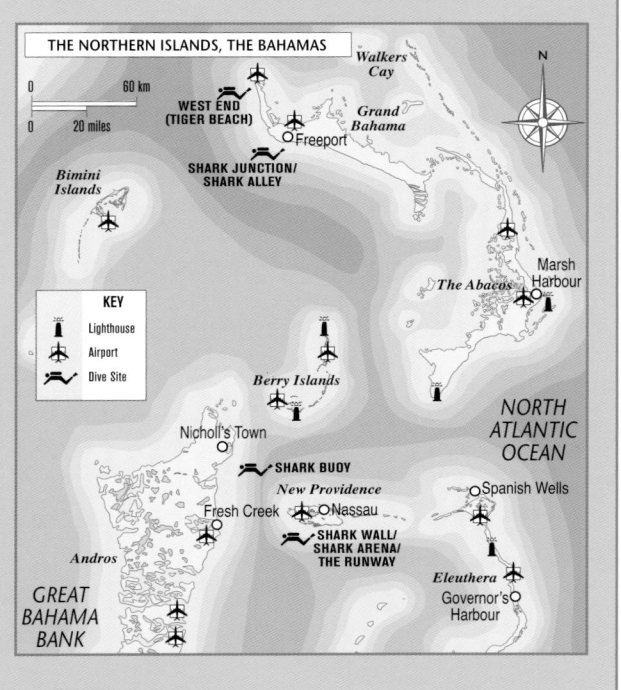

THE NORTHERN ISLANDS, THE BAHAMAS

CLIMATE
Subtropical to tropical, temperatures range from 24°C (75°F) in winter, (December to May), to an average of 28°C (82°F) in summer.

SEASONALITY
Best time is from November – June, avoiding the hurricane season.

GETTING THERE
International carriers fly to Freeport (Grand Bahama) or Nassau through American hubs, then take a local connecting flight. Some live-aboard dive boats operate from Florida.

WATER TEMPERATURE
24°C (75°F) in winter, 29°C (84°F) in summer.

QUALITY OF MARINE LIFE
Very good, the best place in the Caribbean for sharks and dolphins.

DEPTH OF DIVES
Average is 30 m (98 ft); but some places have depths well beyond the accepted limits of sport diving on air.

SAFETY
Suitable for all standards of divers who are not frightened by sharks.

DIVING IN CENOTES
MEXICO

44

The Yucatán Peninsula in southeastern Mexico projects northeastwards from Central America separating the Gulf of Mexico on the west and north from the Caribbean Sea on the east.

The coastline is roughly 1,127 km (700 miles), the average width is 323 km (200 miles) and the area is 197,600 sq km (76,300 sq miles). The region is directly within the hurricane belt, which can cause problems at the popular resorts of Cancún and the island of Cozumel. The Mexican name for the Atlantic coast of the Yucatán Peninsula is Riviera Maya, often called Maya or Mayan Riviera.

The island of Cozumel is about 16 km (10 miles) off the eastern coast of the Yucatán Peninsula, Mexico, and is under the jurisdiction of Quintana Roo. The island is 47 km (29 miles) from northeast to southwest and averages 15 km (9 miles) across. The largest of the islands off the peninsula, it has an area of 489 sq km (189 sq miles).

Most diving takes place in the calmer waters of the leeward, southwest coast of Cozumel where a series of inner and outer reefs parallel to the coastline slow down the currents. Since 1980 a ban on fishing in these waters has protected the reef fish that include southern stingrays, spotted eagle rays, green moray eels, squirrelfish, yellowtail snapper, angelfish, butterflyfish and stoplight parrotfish.

The Yucatán Peninsula is world famous for caves and karst features, the most obvious being cenotes – freshwater pools or sinkholes. The word cenote is derived from the Mayan word *dzonot* and refers to any subterranean chamber that contains permanent water.

Some cenotes are vertical shafts containing water, while others are caves that contain pools and underwater passageways and may be connected to submerged caverns and other cenotes to form long underwater cave systems. Various cenotes have now been connected by cave divers to produce the world's longest cave system. The standard formation visible on land is a round hole in the ground.

Cenotes were formed when a limestone surface collapsed, exposing water underneath. The major source of water in modern and ancient Yucatán, cenotes are also associated with the cult of the rain gods, or Chacs. In ancient times, notably at Chichén Itzá, precious objects, such as jade, gold, copper and incense and also human beings, usually children, were thrown into the cenotes as offerings. A survivor was believed to bring a message from the gods about that year's crops.

Cenotes start out as a solution cavern where acidic groundwater seeps through cracks in the limestone bedrock and dissolves softer limestone lying underneath the hard surface crust. Over time, this process creates large underground caverns roofed with only a thin layer of surface limestone. After further erosion, the thin roof collapses, leaving an open, water-filled hole that fills with organic and mineral debris. Eventually the cenote may fill completely, becoming dry and having trees and other vegetation.

Diving in a cenote can be either cave diving – diving in a cave beyond the reach of natural sunlight, or cavern diving – remaining in sight of the entrance within the range of natural sunlight. When cave diving a diver must be properly equipped and either be a certified cave diver or be accompanied by a certified cave diving divemaster. Most accessible cenotes open to the public

Right Large stalactites hang from the ceiling of a cenote

in Yucatán are equipped with a permanent safety guideline to serve as a reference. Cave and cavern diving courses are available.

CENOTE CAR WASH (AKTUN HA OR WATER CAVE)

Divers can drive to the Car Wash or Aktun Ha (Water Cave). Locals used to wash their vehicles at the Cenote, which is 8 km from Tulum on the road to Coba. It is open 9am–5pm daily, attracts an entry fee and has basic changing and bathroom facilities for use before and after dives.

Due to its easy accessibility, Car Wash is one of the most popular cenotes. The entrance is a huge limestone arch, and the cenote connects to a labyrinth of dark tunnels and caves, but there is debris from fallen trees and leaves, which should be avoided if at all possible. It is suitable for divers of all levels of experience in the cavern section but you are advised to wear a wet or Lycra suit with a hood for protection from small fish such as tetra that may bite. There is a wooden platform and steps so divers can enter the water easily. During the warmer months there is a layer of algae at the water's surface, so snorkelling is best during winter months, when the surface is clearer.

There are upstream and downstream dives. The upstream entrance is to the right, the downstream entrance to the left. Most divers choose to go upstream.

Where the cavern becomes a cave there are warning signs advising divers against going further unless cave certified. Certified cave divers heading upstream can encounter the Chamber of Horrors, Luke's Hope, Crystal Palace and The Room of Tears and then backtrack to Adriana's Room and the Cell Block. The Car Wash is famous for its soda-straw stalactites that grow on the ceilings as delicate, thin-walled hollow tubes, especially in The Room of Tears.

The downstream section requires more caution.

Left A diver swims carefully between stalactites in the Car Wash

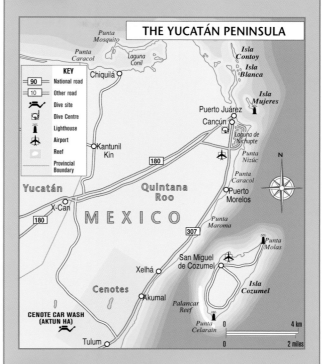

THE YUCATÁN PENINSULA

CLIMATE
Averages 20°C (68°F) in winter, and up to 40°C (105°F) in summer.

SEASONALITY
Best dived from December to June to avoid the hurricane season.

GETTING THERE
International flights to Cancun or connection via the USA.

WATER TEMPERATURE
For reefs 22-24°C (72-75°F) in winter, 24-28°C (75-82°F) in summer. Cenotes average 24-25°C (75-77°F).

QUALITY OF MARINE LIFE
Specialized cave-dwelling animals are found in the cenotes.

DEPTH OF DIVES
From 10-35 m (33-115 ft) and deeper off reefs, the average depth is 9 m (29 ft) in the cavern section of Car Wash.

SAFETY
Cave diving certification or being accompanied by a cave dive certified divemaster is required to dive in caves.

BIG FISH
CUBA

Shaped like a sleeping crocodile, Cuba is the largest island in the Caribbean.

Lying 145 km (90 miles) south of Florida between Jamaica and the Bahamas, Cuba is 1,199 km (745 miles)-long, 35–200 km (22–124 miles)-wide and has a total area of 105,006 sq km (4,054 square miles). Washed by the Atlantic Ocean in the north, the Caribbean Sea to the south and the Gulf of Mexico to the west, its 5,746 km (3,571 mile) coastline teems with fish, making it probably the most prolific diving destination in the Caribbean for animal life. The largest island outside of the main island is the Isla de la Juventud (Isle of Youth) in the southwest, which has an area of 3,056 sq km (1,180 sq miles).

Although the Isla de la Juventud is Cuba's best-known diving region, foreign investment has constructed top-class hotels in other areas where good diving exists. These hotels, together with the introduction of a barge converted into a floating hotel and live-aboard boats opening up the marine park of Los Jardines de la Reina, have placed Cuban diving firmly on the international diving map.

ISLA DE LA JUVENTUD (THE ISLE OF YOUTH)
The largest of Cuba's offshore islands, the Isla de la Juventud has many of Cuba's premier dive sites along its southwest shore. The diving is based on Hotel El Colony on the coast west of Siguanea, but the dive sites are from Cape Francés to Point Pedernales and include a 6 km (4 mile) strip known as the Pirate Coast. Highly organized with a fixed restaurant complex for lunch, there are nearly 60 marked dive sites and fixed moorings to minimize anchor damage. With minimal currents the fish life is profuse, tame and approachable. Punta Francés (Frenchman's Point) is a marine national park.

The island is in a sheltered position off Cuba's southwest coast, protected from both the wind and the waves and is unaffected by the currents from the Gulf of Mexico. The reefs themselves are of superb quality and are frequented by large schools of fish including tarpon and barracuda. The tops of the reefs have gullies and caverns that lead to steep drop-offs plunging to depths of more than 1,000 m (3,281 ft). Giant groupers and shoals of snappers, surgeonfish and grunts can be

Right A French angelfish at Pipín

INVASION OF INDO-PACIFIC LIONFISH
A voracious predator, lionfish introduced into the Tropical Western Atlantic Ocean, (Caribbean) are decimating local fish populations,

A study has found that within a short period after the introduction of Indo-Pacific lionfish into an area, the survival of other reef fishes is lowered by about 80 per cent.

Apart from the death of local fish, the loss of herbivorous fish allows seaweeds to grow over the coral reefs and disrupt the delicate ecological balance of reefs.

It is believed that the first lionfish were introduced into marine waters off Florida in the early 1990s from local aquariums or home aquariums. They have since spread across much of the Caribbean Sea and north along the United States East coast as far as Rhode Island. This invasive species, which is native to the tropical Pacific and Indian Oceans, has few natural enemies to control it in the Atlantic Ocean, and is therefore undergoing a population explosion.

Lionfish can eat other fish up to two-thirds of their own length, while they are protected from predators by long, poisonous spines. Groupers, which eat lionfish in the Pacific Ocean, have been heavily overfished in the Tropical Western Atlantic Ocean.

TROPICAL WESTERN ATLANTIC

found over the reefs as well as under the many arches and overhangs while deeper waters have eagle rays, turtles and the occasional reef shark.

Some sites are at 30 m (98 ft) with valleys descending to between 50 and 80 m (164 and 262 ft). The reefs are forested with gorgonian sea fans, sea plumes and sea rods and bowl, tube, vase and octopus sponges.

Large shoals of tarpon barely condescend to move aside as divers swim through them. Barracuda, rainbow runners, trumpetfish, red snappers, schoolmaster snappers and yellowtail snappers follow them around. Spiny lobsters, batwing coral crabs and green moray eels abound and stingrays are found on the sand. The myriad of friendly fish include queen angelfish, French angelfish, queen triggerfish, sargassum triggerfish, black durgon, ocean surgeonfish, blue tangs, butterflyfish, grunts, groupers, Spanish hogfish, parrotfish and scrawled filefish.

LOS JARDINES DE LA REINA
Known to Americans as Lost Paradise Keys, Los Jardines de la Reina (The Gardens of the Queen) are

good enough to attract discerning divers and most of the dive sites are protected from the winds and currents. The archipelago stretches for over 161 km (100 miles) and is some 80 km (50 miles) offshore south of mainland Cuba and 129 km (80 miles) north of Cayman Brac. Since 1996 the archipelago has been the largest Caribbean marine park with an area of 2,170 sq km (838 sq miles). Access is restricted: there are no civilians living on any of the islands in the national park and commercial fishing is banned. Only scuba diving and sport-fishing are allowed. The archipelago is only accessible by water through the mainland port of Júcaro.

The fish fauna here is the best in Cuba for richness, density and the size of the larger species, with almost twice the biomass and density than any other Cuban sub-archipelago and three times more than any other Caribbean island.

As well as the smaller reef fish there are massive goliath groupers, shoals of tarpon, snappers and jacks and lone green moray eels. The larger species include silky, blacktip reef, Caribbean reef, lemon, nurse, bull

Below Tarpon usually shoal together

and occasionally shoals of scalloped hammerhead sharks. Whale sharks are often encountered late in the year. There are over 80 dive sites along hundreds of small cays with mangrove nurseries teeming with reef fish including huge barracuda and groupers. The islands are well-known for their turtle population; four species of marine turtles: loggerheads, hawksbills, leatherbacks and greens can be found.

South of Cayo Caballones, Pipín has sandy gullies among brain and star corals on a gentle slope from 15-22 m (49-72 ft). Named after the freediver Pipín Ferreras, this site has a large swim-through at 40 m (131 ft). Divers can see large, goliath groupers, tarpon and yellowtail snappers. Silky sharks are often seen if the water has been chummed. West of Cayo Anclitas, Avalon has abundant fish life at 37 m (121 ft) that attracts blacktip reef, bull and silky sharks. Southeast of Cayo Anclitas, Meseta de los Meros is particularly known for its groupers down to 32 m (105 ft). Southeast of Cayo Anclitas, La Cueva del Pulpo (Octopus Cave) is best known for large pillar corals, a cave, octopuses and goliath groupers, and to the southeast, Cabezo de Coral Negro is known for blacktip reef, bull and occasionally silky sharks at 35-40 m (115-131 ft). The dive takes place just above a coral shelf at 38 m (125 ft) where the divers watch the shark activity, or go slightly deeper to look at the black coral formations that give the site its name.

FACTS

CLIMATE
Semitropical with two seasons, up to 26°C (80°F) from December to March, rising to 32°C (90°F) in July and August. Humidity and rainfall are highest in September/October.

SEASONALITY
Diving is possible all year round though slightly rougher seas are encountered in winter. The best visibility is from the end of December until May. Hurricanes are possible between August and November. August, September and November are the months when divers are most likely to see whale sharks.

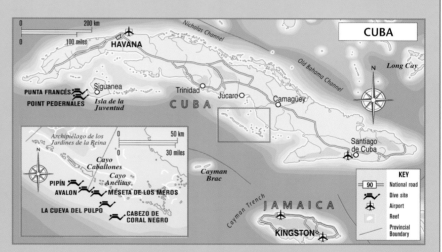

GETTING THERE
Direct flights to José Martí International Airport in Havana.
Isla de la Juventud: A 25-minute flight connects to Rafael Cabrera Mustelier Airport, Nueva Gerona wherea 40 km (25 miles) drive by road takes you to the El Colony Diving Complex.
Los Jardines de la Reina: From Havana either travel by road to Júcaro or fly to Cayo Coco and travel on by road to Júcaro. Transfer from Júcaro to Los Jardines de la Reina is included in dive packages.

American citizens should check their latest government advisory information before to travelling to Cuba.

WATER TEMPERATURE
Average 28°C (82°F) in summer, 24°C (75°F) in winter.

QUALITY OF MARINE LIFE
Diverse and prolific, and apart from sharks it is tame and approachable.

DEPTH OF DIVES
Usually shallow, generally less than 30 m (98 ft), but there are some sites that require short decompression stops and others that descend deeper than sports divers should dive – act responsibly.

SAFETY
Cuban diving is mostly relaxed and suitable for all standards of divers except on deeper dives.

BIG FISH, CUBA

STINGRAYS
CAYMAN ISLANDS

Situated in the western Caribbean, the British Overseas Territory of the Cayman Islands consists of Grand Cayman, Cayman Brac and Little Cayman, 773 km (480 miles) south of Miami, Florida, 241 Km (150 miles) south of Cuba and 290 km (180 miles) northwest of Jamaica.

Cayman Brac and Little Cayman are located roughly 129 km (80 miles) east of Grand Cayman. The islands were formed by large coral heads covering submerged seamounts that are western extensions of the Cuban Sierra Maestra range.

The Cayman Islands were one of the first recreational diving destinations in the Caribbean, with Bob Soto opening Grand Cayman's first dive shop in 1957. However, although the diving is still as good as it was, the Cayman Islands have been declining in diver popularity after a combination of damage from hurricanes and a series of ill-advised decisions by local officials and tourism promoters allowing large numbers of cruise ship passenger numbers on the shallow reefs.

The Department of Tourism, recognizing that development has killed many of the reefs off Grand Cayman's Seven Mile Beach, hopes to scuttle the de-commissioned World War II United States Navy submarine rescue ship USS *Kittiwake* off the north end of Seven Mile Beach to add to the purposely sunk MV *Captain Keith Tibbets*.

Right The silhouettes of a stingray and a diver at Stingray City

Overpage A majestic manta ray cruising over a reef

52

TROPICAL WESTERN ATLANTIC

STINGRAY BARBS

Stingrays can be among the largest of venomous fish, varying in size from a few centimetres to several metres. The tail of the stingray carries at least one barb or spine that may be up to 37 cm (14 inches)-long on top of the tail. Each barb is covered by a film of venom and mucous. These barbs point backwards, but can be used in any direction. The rays thrash out when surprised, trodden on, swam over closely or caught.

Stingray injuries mostly occur when a person steps on a ray. The stingray whips its tail around, lacerating the foot or lower leg, sometimes leaving some of the barb in the wound. With large stingrays, the mechanical injury can be severe, with fatal cases due to directly piercing the heart, bowel or a major artery. In the same way that people with knife wounds to the heart are advised to leave the knife in place until a surgeon can try to remove it, those suffering from barbs piercing the heart should not compound the wound by pulling out the barb; it is important to leave the barb in place and get the victim to surgical expertise in a hospital as soon as possible. Removing the barb without relevant expertise is likely to worsen the bleeding.

For smaller stingrays, like most other fish toxins the venom is a large molecular weight protein that can be broken down by heat. First aid should begin with immersion of the wound in hot but non-scalding water. Clean the wound, apply a broad ligature or pressure bandage between the limb and the body. Immerse the limb in hot water at 50°C (122°F) for between 30-minutes and 2 hours, until the pain stops. The cooling water from an outboard motor has been used when no other supply of hot water was available. Release the ligature every 15-minutes to allow blood to flow into the limb. Several injections of local anaesthetic, around the wound site will ease the pain if they are available. The young or weak may need cardiac or respiratory resuscitation if the heart or breathing stops.

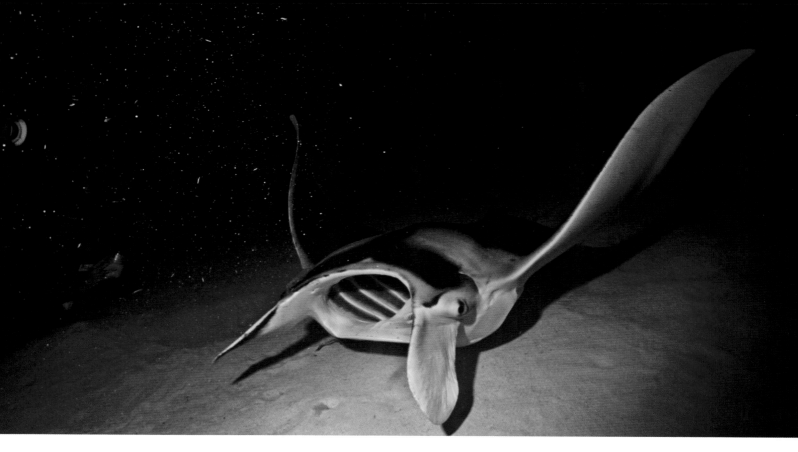

Above A mata ray cruises along the sea bed

The Cayman Islands do not have any rivers to give run-off and the Caribbean's greatest known depth, the Cayman Trench, also known as the Bartlett Deep or Bartlett Trough, comes close to the shore in places. The lack of run-off and the trench are responsible for the higher than average water clarity as the sediment descends into the deep. The drop-off starts its descent as a wall approximately 91 m (100 yards) from shore where depths range from 12-18 m (40-60 ft).

STINGRAY CITY – GRAND CAYMAN

Grand Cayman's Stingray City is probably dived or snorkelled by more people than any other site in the world. The site lies just inside a natural channel passing through the barrier reef on the northwest corner of Grand Cayman's North Sound. 3.5-5.5 m (12-18 ft)-deep, it is flat sand with solitary coral heads so it is an ideal place for stingrays to search for food in the sand. Cayman fishermen used to anchor in this sheltered spot to clean their catch before landing it; they threw the waste

overboard and over the years, stingrays became accustomed to this plentiful supply of food.

Discovered by divers in summer 1986, an American diving magazine sent a journalist down in 1987 and she coined the name 'Stingray City', while her editor invented the headline 'The World's Best 3.5 m (12 ft) Dive'. Nowadays there is also a similar site called 'The Sandbar' near Rum Point channel, which is only waist deep.

At Stingray City southern stingrays follow the sound of any approaching boat engine and as soon as it is anchored they converge from all directions seeking a free lunch. The dive can be slightly frightening as the stingrays nudge and jostle people boisterously in their search for food.

Adult female stingrays can be 2 m (6.6 ft)-across but most animals found here are smaller males. Searching for their prey in the sand they have eyes on the top of their bodies but their mouths are set back underneath. They cannot see their prey, but sense food with highly developed receptors, smell and touch, sucking food into their mouths between two hard dental plates. They are often confused by the scent of several people carrying food in the water and begin sucking as they approach what they think is the source of the food. This can result in uncomfortable 'hickies' – suction marks on divers skin similar to love bites. For this reason, and the high chance of sunburn in such shallow water, it is wise to wear a Lycra skin suit or light wetsuit.

Boat skippers provide clients with pieces of chopped up squid and if they keep the food in their closed fist the rays can be led around following the scent, though people may get jostled by another stingray approaching from another direction. When divers wish to feed the stingrays, they should open their fist and keep their fingers straight, pointed away from the hand so that their palm is flat and bent backwards. The stingrays do not have teeth but can generate the suction of a vacuum cleaner. Stingrays are bottom dwellers, feeding primarily on molluscs and crustaceans in the sand so one cannot just release the fish into the water as the stingrays cannot catch it. If divers do release the bait into the water it is most likely to be snapped up by yellowtail snappers or sergeant majors.

Once the feeding session is over the rays slow down and become more docile, this is a good time to take photographs if the sand is not stirred up too much.

FACTS

CLIMATE
Fine weather year-round. Summer temperatures average 30-40°C (86-105°F) dropping to a low of 20°C (68°F) during the winter season. Warm, rainy summers (May to October) and cool, relatively dry winters (November to April)

SEASONALITY
Best May-September although dive operators boast that you can dive every day of the year as there is always a lee coast. The official Caribbean hurricane season is June to November and tends to be worst in the Cayman Islands in September to November.

GETTING THERE
International flights to Owen Roberts International Airport, 3 km (2 miles) east of George Town on Grand Cayman and Gerrard Smith Airport 8 km (5 miles) from West End on Cayman Brac, with local flights connecting to all three islands including Edward Bodden Airfield on Little Cayman.

WATER TEMPERATURE
Average 27°C (80°F) during winter; 28°C (82°F) in summer.

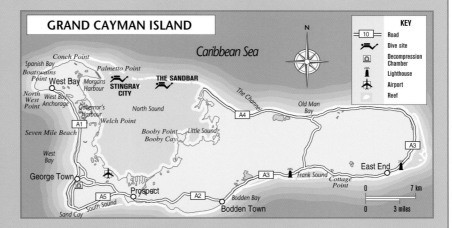

QUALITY OF MARINE LIFE
Above average for the Caribbean. Large shoals of fish, turtles, manta rays and of course, stingrays.

DEPTH OF DIVES
From the surface to 5.5 m (18 ft) for the stingrays.

SAFETY
Suitable for all standards of diver. It is recommended that all participants wear some form of protective clothing against suction bruises ('Hickies') from the stingrays' mouths and sunburn. Those who prefer to only watch should fold their arms across their chests with each hand under the opposite arm. Those who do not like being bumped around should move back from the divers who are feeding the stingrays or watch from the surface. These animals are not aggressive but do not pull their tails as they have venomous barbs for defence, which can inflict a painful wound. Do not wear gloves as the fabric can remove protective mucous from the stingrays' skin exposing them to infection.

ARTIFICIAL REEFS

Artificial reefs in shallow waters are a well proven, successful way of enhancing fish stocks. Shipwrecks rapidly take on the appearance of a reef. They form a good substratum for coral larvae to settle on, provide shelter for bigger fish and breeding sites for smaller fish and invertebrates.

Purposely sunk reefs are now common. For many years, disused ships, aircraft, railway carriages and car bodies have been environmentally cleaned and then sunk as artificial reefs.

REEF BALLS

In times gone by concrete slabs or small concrete pyramids were linked together to form artificial reefs. A modern version is the use of environmentally-friendly concrete 'Reef Balls' seeded with coral-fragments to form artificial reefs. Reef Balls were designed in America by the Reef Ball Development Group Limited, a non-profit organisation helping to restore the world's ocean ecosystem. They have been used successfully in several parts of Southeast Asia where they also deter fishing-trawlers from illegal trawling by ripping their nets and thus helping to protect marine turtles.

Reef balls are formed in fibreglass moulds, using cement that contains silica and has a similar pH to natural seawater; they do not contain toxins or biologically active compounds. They remain stable on the sea bottom even in hurricanes because they are dense, of moderate to low profile and designed in such a way that more than half of their weight is on the base of the ball on the seabed. They have rough surface textures and have holes in them to create vortexes. The large space in the centre provides shelter for fish while the surfaces enhance the settlement of marine life.

Reef balls usually resemble pyramids rather than balls; they come in different sizes, ranging from 15 cm (6 inches) to nearly 2m (6ft).

People experimenting with coral propagation have developed a way to transplant pieces of fragmented coral on to the reef ball to give the coral a good start for growth.

The mould consists of three main fibreglass pieces held together with pins. Silica in the cement helps to give the reef balls an expected life of 500 years or more.

If a piece of coral is broken off the main growth but is still alive it can be saved if it is placed in a stable location where it will not get shifted around and where it will not touch other corals.

ELECTRIC REEFS

Another method makes use of electrolysis. A low voltage direct current is applied to a submerged conductive (metal) structure. Completely safe for swimmers and marine life, this clears any rust and causes dissolved minerals in seawater to precipitate out and accumulate on the metal as a composite of stony limestone and softer brucite (magnesium hydroxide). Adjusting the current and turning it off periodically controls the amount of brucite.

Once minerals coat the metal surface, live stony coral fragments from other reefs are wired to the metal and these bond to the accreted substrate and begin growing three to five times faster than normal, even in stressful conditions. Scientists are not fully sure of the long-term effect of this system but in the short-term it is successful.

Any artificial or re-seeded reef is unlikely to exactly replicate a natural one. Small differences will alter the balance of ecological competition between reef organisms so the final make-up of creatures may differ, but any living reef gives home and protection to a myriad of marine creatures.

Left An artificial reef at Mabul Island off Sabah, Malaysia

CORAL REEFS
ARUBA, BONAIRE AND CURAÇAO

25-80 km (15-50 miles) north of Venezuela, the Islands of Aruba, Bonaire and Curaçao lie from west to east as Aruba, Bonaire and Curaçao (the ABCs).

Usuallly outside of the hurricane belt they are true all-year-round destinations. In the autumn, Coral Spawning is a big event on all three islands.

32 km (20 miles) north of Venezuela, Aruba is the most Americanized of the three islands, it is 33 km (21 miles)-long, 4 km (2.5 miles)-wide and has an area of 193 sq km (75 sq miles). With the best beaches of the three islands, Aruba is for those who want plenty of other activities for non-diving partners or family. Serious divers should avoid the peak cruise ship months of December and January when the most popular sites become crowded.

Curaçao is much larger than Aruba and Bonaire and has more variety both on land and underwater with plenty to occupy non-diving companions. 65 km (40 miles) north of Venezuela, 41 km (26 miles) west of Bonaire and 77 km (48 miles) southeast of Aruba, Curaçao is 61 km (38 miles)-long with a maximum width of 14 km (9 miles) and has an area of 444 sq km (172 sq miles).

The typical fringing reef is a shallow reef shelf in 5-12 m (16-39ft) of water, a drop-off, with a 45° slope or less, then sand shelving into the deep. The reef is steeper at sites in the middle and east of the island. Generally, the best shore diving is in the north, while in the south the drop-offs are steeper with depths of 40 m (131 ft) and are usually less than 150 m (492 ft) from shore.

The entire western side of the island is one large dive site. The stretch from West Point to the Light Tower on Cape Saint Marie is called Bando Abao Underwater Park and that from Bullen Bay to the Princess Beach Hotel is called Central Curaçao Underwater Park. These two parks are voluntary but the stretch from the Princess Beach to East Point has been officially declared Curaçao Underwater Park.

Conditions at the northwestern sites are calm while the southeast has less shelter from the rough seas and currents that produce healthy corals and lush gorgonias. The access points to the island's major shore diving sites are marked with numbered white stones, similar to the yellow ones on Bonaire.

Bonaire vies with Grand Cayman and Cozumel as the top Caribbean destination for American divers. The easternmost island in the ABC group, 80 km (50 miles) north of Venezuela, it is 48 km (30 miles) east of Curaçao and 138 km (86 miles) east of Aruba. The main island is roughly 39 km (24 miles)-long and 8 km (5 miles)-wide at its widest point. The land area is 288 sq km (111 sq miles), while the additional island of Klein Bonaire is a further 6 sq km (2.3 sq miles).

A world leader in the preservation of underwater resources, the whole island is a marine park. Two areas have been designated marine reserves where no diving is allowed, north from Boca Kayon to Boca Slagbaai, and west of Karpata. Lac Bay is protected because of its mangroves and sea-grass beds and heavily dived sites are closed off sporadically to allow recovery. Divers must attend an orientation session and purchase a Marine Park Tag before diving on Bonaire. This tag lasts for one year and is not transferable. Mainland Bonaire has a system of roads with yellow-painted rocks marking the access points for shore-dive sites. Boat dives are organized several times a day to all of the popular sites and this is the only way to dive the sites of Klein Bonaire.

Right Cup corals coat the interior of the wheelhouse of the *Superior Producer*
Overpage A princess parrotfish at Watamula

TROPICAL WESTERN ATLANTIC

Most of Bonaire's diving takes place on the leeward southern and western coasts. The coastline consists of coral rubble or sand beaches down to a drop-off from 5–12 m (16–39 ft) to 40m+ (131 ft+). In the centre of the southern section, between Punt Vierkant and Salt Pier, there is a double-reef system referred to as the Alice in Wonderland double-reef complex. The reef slope is at a shallow angle and descends to a sandy channel at 20-30 m (66-98 ft), and there is a second reef on the other side. On Klein Bonaire buttresses and steep reef slopes are dominant. On

the windward, eastern side of the island there is a shelf and then a drop-off 12 m (39 ft) from the shore, this descends to a coral shelf at 30 m (98 ft) and then drops down to the ocean floor. The sea here is rough for most of the year but often calms down in October or November.

CURAÇAO – WATAMULA

The reefs on Curaçao see fewer divers and have slightly more variation in topography than those on Bonaire, but in general the organisms encountered are

Below A porcupine pufferfish at Bonaire's town pier

Overpage A diver watches a lone turtle swimming above SS *Thistlegorm*

much the same. Bluespotted cornetfish are more common in the shallows, and as divers get deeper the stony corals, sponges and gorgonias become denser, sheltering a multitude of invertebrates. Watamula site is not dived as often as Mushroom Forest because it can be subject to rough seas spreading around the north point from the windward side of the island. However when it is in good condition, this is probably Curaçao's finest reef dive.

Located just south of the north point on the western, leeward side of the island, Watamula is similar to Mushroom Forest but even more lush and overgrown. The seabed is a gentle slope covered in star and brain corals, gorgonian sea whips, sea plumes and sea fans thriving in the nutrient-rich waters. The anemones and vase, basket and tube sponges shelter a multitude of fish and invertebrates. The area is rich in fish life, including snappers, jacks, triggerfish, eagle rays, green moray eels, spotted drums, rock beauties, whitespotted filefish, porcupine pufferfish, snappers, groupers, parrotfish, soldierfish, bluespotted cornetfish, hawksbill turtles, spiny lobsters and banded coral shrimps. Even manta rays and whale sharks have been seen occasionally.

The sea floor is quite confusing so divers should either navigate by compass or drift with the current while the boat follows their bubbles.

This is an exposed area that can sometimes have fairly strong currents in which case it is best treated as a drift-dive, depths descend beyond 40 m (131 ft).

FACTS

CLIMATE
Sunshine on most days except from December to February. The constant trade winds produce an arid desert climate for the rest of the year with the hottest months being August to October. The lowest temperatures are around 24°C (75°F), the hottest rarely go above 32°C (90°F) and the average is 28°C (82°F) with a cooling breeze.

SEASONALITY
The protected west coasts of the ABCs allow diving all year, the more exposed sites are best dived in the summer and autumn.

GETTING THERE
KLM Dutch Airways flies direct from Amsterdam with connections all over Europe. American Airlines and others have connections from several Caribbean countries and North and Latin American gateways while local airlines connect between Curaçao and Bonaire.

WATER TEMPERATURE
24°C (75°F) in the cool season but the average is 27°C (80°F)

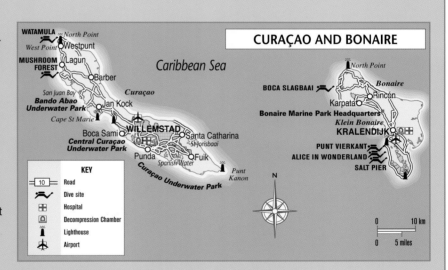

CURAÇAO AND BONAIRE

KEY
10 Road
Dive site
Hospital
Decompression Chamber
Lighthouse
Airport

QUALITY OF MARINE LIFE
Diverse and Prolific, tame and approachable.

DEPTH OF DIVES
Often shallow, generally less than 40 m (131 ft) but drop-offs and walls may descend to depths beyond the accepted limits of sport diving on air.

SAFETY
Except on their windy north and northeast coasts, diving in the ABCs is mostly relaxed and suitable for all standards of divers except on deeper dives. Some dives have moderate currents where intermediate skills are preferable.

DOLPHIN REEF
ISRAEL

For most divers, encounters with dolphins are little more than a fleeting glimpse as a group pass noisily overhead, but some dolphins have accepted the close presence of people in the water.

Most habituated dolphins are bottlenose dolphins, either captive or semi-captive, and these have got used to divers' noisy exhaust bubbles. Where lone dolphins seek out swimmers and snorkellers in harbours or around coasts, these are usually males looking for company, they may have been evicted by their pod but we will never know.

Around the world, various pools, enclosures, amusement parks and dolphinariums have been set up with captive dolphins either for people to pet or to give displays. Fortunately there are a few of these facilities with slightly better intentions where the dolphins are given more room and the freedom to choose whether or not they interact with human beings. These dolphins are usually ones that have been rescued from shows and their offspring so interaction with human beings is normal to them. As dolphins are considered 'cuddly and calming', these facilities also offer dolphin-assisted therapeutic sessions.

One such facility is Dolphin Reef in the Gulf of Aqaba (Gulf of Eilat), in Israel. 1 km (0.6 miles) south of Eilat, Dolphin Reef is 10,000-Sq. metre (107,639-Sq. ft) of sea, which averages 12 m (39 ft)-deep and is enclosed with buoyed nets. The maximum depth is 18 m (59 ft).

The enclosure houses a group of bottlenose dolphins (*Tursiops truncatus*) from the Black Sea together with their offspring who were born at Dolphin Reef. The dolphins can jump the net to freedom and often do, returning later with fresh propeller scars on their backs. The enclosure also contains a wooden wreck and reef fish including some interesting species rescued from fishermen such as cobia and large habituated stingrays. Sea lions from a smaller enclosure beside the dolphin enclosure regularly jump the net to join in with the fun.

Some experts believe that patients suffering from depression and mental illness experience an uplifting effect when they swim with dolphins so Dolphin Reef is fully equipped to deal with those that are emotionally challenged or those who have other special needs, including the blind and those normally confined to wheelchairs.

Divers feel privileged to get so close to the dolphins at Dolphin Reef. They enter the enclosure full of anticipation, they can hear the clicks and shrieks of the dolphins' echolocation – but at first they cannot see them. Suddenly two or more dolphins will speed into view, a vision of graceful beauty rushing up to the divers and coming to a halt, peering quizzically into their face masks, just inches away from their faces and seemingly posing for the divers cameras.

Recognizing the accompanying staff divemaster, they will search him or her for food.

After tiring of playing, they will move away, but soon dash back again, passing by and then beneath the divemaster, twisting onto their backs and inviting him to scratch their stomachs. More dolphins suddenly arrive and begin to interact, playfully twirling and tumbling around with lots of noise, touching each other or nosing each other's fins. Some dolphins burrow in the sand for prey, mothers suckle their calves, while others play with bits of seaweed, passing it to each other – and even to the divers, as if asking them to join in the fun.

Right Two bottlenose dolphins get up close and personal

INDIAN OCEAN

It is impossible to know what a dolphin is thinking about when it peers into a diver's face-mask. Is it looking at its own reflection? Is it treating the diver as a friend, or is it using echolocation on a frequency that you cannot hear to 'look' deeper into your body as it does through the sand in the quest for prey? There have been several recorded cases where lone male bottlenose dolphins have sought out human company and reacted sexually, so it is likely that their response to interaction with swimmers and divers is favourable so long as the animals are not harassed.

Dolphins have always been perceived as 'cuddly' creatures, although recent research has found that some dolphin species kill smaller species.

Each day at Dolphin Reef the dolphins see hundreds of divers and snorkellers, so they could be forgiven for becoming bored with them; it is best to book the first dive of the day for the best visibility and when the dolphins have not had human contact overnight so they are likely to be more curious.

Guided dives with the dolphins at Dolphin Reef are available to all qualified divers with a logged dive within the last six months and valid local diving insurance. Dives take place in groups with a maximum of four persons plus a member of staff and the dive time is 30 to 35-minutes. When a dolphin approaches a diver, it does so out of its own free will.

Snorkellers enter the enclosure by swimming over the net but divers enter through a sliding curtain facing the shore at the seabed. The dolphins sense the noise of this curtain being opened and immediately appear at high speed with lots of clicking and shrieking. Once they have had a quick inspection of the newcomers, and searched the accompanying staff for titbits of food they go back to their boisterous play.

There are those who object to habituating wild animals or keeping them in enclosures, but the dolphins are not forced to interact with mankind and for children, particularly, the creatures of Dolphin Reef provide instill a strong message of conservation.

Left A bottlenose dolphin interacts with a member of staff at Dolphin Reef

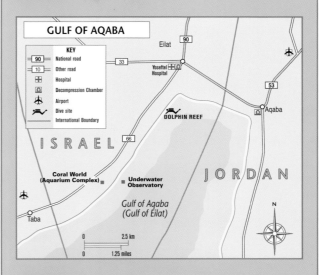

FACTS

CLIMATE
Warm, mostly dry winters, average 20ºC (68ºF). Hot, dry summers, average 35ºC (95ºF).

SEASONALITY
All year round but best April-August. It can be cold in winter.

GETTING THERE
Eilat airport only handles small aircraft, so some divers fly to Tel Aviv and then go to Eilat by road. International charter flights use the military airport at Ovda, 40-minutes by road from Eilat. Then travel to Dolphin Reef by road.

WATER TEMPERATURE
Summer average 25ºC (77ºF), 19ºC (66ºF) in winter when a thick wetsuit or a dry-suit are preferable.

QUALITY OF MARINE LIFE
Dolphins and a few reef and pelagic fish.

DEPTH OF DIVES
From the surface to 14 m (46 ft).

SAFETY
Very safe for all standards of diver.

THE SS *THISTLEGORM*
EGYPT

The SS *Thistlegorm* may not be the best wreck in the world but due to of its easy accessibility and contents, it has become one of the most dived; resembling a World War II army surplus store. Many who dive on the wreck act like children in a candy shop. Since its rediscovery in 1992, diver traffic has taken its toll.

Thistlegorm translates as 'Blue Thistle'. 4,976 tonnes, 126.5 m (415 ft)-long, 18 m (59 ft)-beam and 7.45 m (24 ft)-draft, the vessel was powered by a triple-expansion, three-cylinder engine. On her last voyage she set off laden with supplies for the Western Desert Force in North Africa.

The Germans and Italians controlled most of the Mediterranean so the *Thistlegorm* sailed the long way round the Cape of Good Hope and was escorted up the Red Sea to Suez. She was waiting with other ships at a Sha'b 'Ali anchorage for clearance to enter the Suez Canal but two vessels had collided further up the Gulf of Suez and were blocking the route. Unfortunately two German Heinkel He-111 bombers failed to find their main target, so they jettisoned their bombs on the *Thistlegorm* instead. Early on October 6th 1941 two bombs penetrated No. 5 hold, aft of the *Thistlegorm*'s bridge. The aft holds contained the ordnance of the *Thistlegorm* and the resulting explosions ripped a huge hole in the aft section and sent the two locomotives on the deck spiralling into the air as the ship was ripped open. The vessel was set on fire and soon sank, four of the merchant seamen and five of the Royal Navy

personnel on board to man the guns were killed. The survivors were rescued by HMS *Carlisle* but as was the custom at the time, the surviving crew's pay was stopped and they had to make their own way home.

Poorly-marked on the charts, the wreck remained undisturbed until the early fifties when Jacques-Yves Cousteau's team on their vessel *Calypso* found her. This was reported in the February 1956 edition of *National Geographic* magazine and the film and book *The Living Sea*. At that time amateur diving was not common in the Red Sea and Cousteau's team never gave the wreck's coordinates, so the *Thistlegorm* was forgotten until a British wreck fanatic began asking the right questions.

Local fishermen are always likely to know the

Right A turtle glides above SS *Thistlegorm*

FIXED MOORINGS ON THE *THISTLEGORM*

As the SS *Thistlegorm* was suffering considerable damage due to the number and size of diving vessels being irresponsibly tied to it, especially in strong currents, the Hurghada Environmental Protection and Conservation Association, (HEPCA), has installed fixed and buoyed mooring lines to protect the wreck. Initially these were not considered successful for all sizes of vessel but after modifications a working system was found and all vessels must now use these moorings. In addition, boats are no longer permitted to use the mooring system unless they also have a stern anchor. The extra stability given by a stern anchor should help to ensure that the lines do not become shredded by rubbing against the structure of the wreck in wind and strong currents.

HEPCA also drilled some holes in the wreck to allow trapped air to escape.

positions of wrecks because they are either good line fishing or they snag and destroy their nets. In October 1992, local Bedouin fishermen told an Israeli charter boat captain, Shimshon Machiah, about a good site for fishing and he informed other Israeli captains – the *Thistlegorm* was rediscovered.

Not quite as good a dive as the *Umbria* in Sudan because the visibility is often poor and the currents can be strong, the *Thistlegorm* was laden with military equipment from Bedford trucks loaded with BSA and Norton motorcycles, an armoured Rolls Royce, Bren guns, vehicle and aircraft parts, gun carriers, munitions and two railway locomotives to Lee Enfield rifles, radios and Wellington Boots.

Today the *Thistlegorm* lies to the northeast of Shag Rock, east of the southern end of Sha'b 'Ali in the straits of Gubal (27° 49' N / 33° 55' E). She is almost upright, slightly listing to port except for the stern section, which is broken away and lies heavily to port. The bottom of the bow is at 30 m (98 ft), the propeller and rudder are at 32 m (105 ft) and the superstructure rises to 12 m (39 ft). The locomotives were thrown to either side of the vessel. Conditions vary with a current from medium to strong. Get there early in the early morning and she is still a tremendous dive, and the holds contain all the implements of war. In the early days toolkits could be found under the seats of the motorcycles but nowadays hordes of divers have removed artefacts, the toolkits, badges, pedals and twist-grips are all gone and only a few of the vehicles' steering wheels remain. Penetration is easy around the bridge and blast area. The large prop is still in position and the guns on the stern are visible. A bath can be seen towards the bow and a toilet near to the stern. The hull is covered with stony and Dendronephthya soft tree corals, sponges and most species of Egyptian Red Sea reef fish. Nurse sharks, large groupers and turtles rest among the wreckage and the handrails are covered in corals and sponges.

Left Motorcycles make up some of the military cargo in the holds of the SS *Thistlegorm*

FACTS

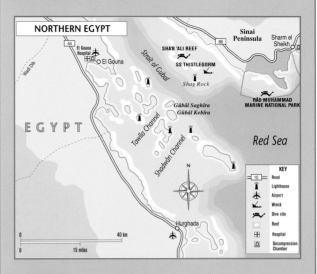

CLIMATE
Warm, mostly dry winters, average 20ºC (68ºF), but cold and windy out to sea. Hot, dry summers average 35ºC (95ºF), but the winds at sea can be strong. Have warm clothes available if on a boat. Divers are only exposed to the heat ashore when travelling on land.

SEASONALITY
All year round, but best April-August, it can be cold and rough in winter.

GETTING THERE
Fly to Sharm el Sheikh or to Cairo and then by road to Sharm el Sheikh, then by boat.

WATER TEMPERATURE
Summer average 25ºC (77ºF), 19ºC (66ºF) in winter when a thick wetsuit or a dry-suit are preferable.

QUALITY OF MARINE LIFE
Very good, a high density of stony and soft corals, gorgonias, other invertebrates and both reef and pelagic fish including Sharks.

DEPTH OF DIVES
From 15-33 m (49-108 ft) on the wreck.

SAFETY
Currents are strong and can be fierce.

SHARK AND JOLANDA REEFS
EGYPT

When sport diving began off the Sinai, one of the first good sites discovered was Shark/Jolanda Reef off Râs Muhammad at the southern tip of the Sinai.

Divers did not realize that they had found one of the best dives in the whole Red Sea. In those days almost all diving was done from the shore and divers came here to experience sharks. Along with the SS *Thistlegorm*, these two reefs are the signature dives of Egypt. Nowadays there are too many divers so the sharks at Shark Reef have become bored with them and descended into deeper water, whitetip reef sharks are still regularly found in caves deep down but the other sharks, including grey reef, blacktip reef and tiger sharks, tend to remain on the limit of visibility although they are seen more at night or in winter when the water is colder.

There is access to the reefs from the beach for snorkellers and shore divers and there are also mooring sites for boats. However, because of strong currents the reef is now usually dived by boat and must be the most heavily dived site in the Red Sea.

The name Râs Muhammad appeared on Spanish maps as early as 1762 and literally means 'Muhammad's Head', where 'head' in this instance means headland, cape or point. There is a saying in the area that in side view the contour of the cliff looks like the profile of a bearded man's face.

Rising from deep water off Râs Muhammad's southern tip and separated from the mainland by a shallow channel are the two peaks of a single seamount that is swept by strong currents. These peaks sit on an underwater ledge over an extremely deep drop-off. The most northeasterly of these is called Shark Reef after its sharks and the more southwesterly one is called Jolanda Reef after a wreck that sank here during a violent storm in 1980. The two peaks are about 40-50 m (131-164 ft)-apart and are connected by a shallow 15–20 m (49-66 ft) saddle. Shark Reef is the most interesting for species and Jolanda is the larger reef of the two.

The reefs are part of Egypt's first protected area – The Râs Muhammad Marine National Park, which is managed by the Egyptian Environmental Affairs Agency (EEAA). The park is situated at the southern extreme of the Sinai Peninsula, overlooking the Gulf of Suez to the west and the Gulf of Aqaba to the east. Originally established in

Right A diver and a yellowbar angelfish over the *Jolanda*'s deck cargo

MAGNIFYING GLASSES AND THEIR USE UNDERWATER

With any lens, rays of light are bent when they cross from the surrounding medium into the glass or plastic of a magnifying glass and then again when they pass through the other side of the lens. In simple terms, the amount of bending and hence magnification depends on the change of refractive index as the light enters and then leaves the magnifying glass.

Underwater, the change of refractive index is less than it would be in air so the amount of magnification is less. However, divers and snorkellers already have an answer to this problem with the air space trapped behind their facemask. Because light has to travel through water, glass, and air before it enters the diver's eye it creates a magnification; objects appear to be larger and closer than they actually are. What divers require is a magnifying glass that is sealed within its own airspace. Some muck divers manufacture their own but there is also a Dutchman, J. S. Schulte, who markets these on the web.

1983, this national park includes the islands of Tiran and Sanafir to the east and now covers an area of 480 sq km (184 Sq miles), including 135 sq km (52 Sq miles) of land and 345 sq km (133 Sq miles) over water.

More than 200 species of corals are found in the Râs Muhammad area including 125 species of soft corals. In addition there are more than 1000 species of fishes, 40 species of star fishes, 25 species of sea urchins, more than a 100 species of molluscs and 150 species of crustaceans. Green and hawksbill turtles are seen regularly.

Off the ledge, the seaward sides of both reefs drop as near vertical walls to depths deeper than sport divers should dive on air. A small flat plateau on the outside and west of Jolanda Reef is littered with cargo from the wreck of the Cypriot freighter *Jolanda* (pronounced Yolanda), which was sailing from Cape Town to Aqaba when it went aground in a storm, these include the metal skeletons of containers, RSJs, cables, earthenware toilets, sinks, rolls of linoleum and shower curtains. If divers look hard there is even a BMW car though little is left of it other than a couple of wheels and tyres, clutch

Below Diver, anthias and mixed corals at Shark Reef, Râs Muhammad

and brake pedals. The actual hull of the ship slipped into deep water during another storm in 1986 and is now a deep dive between 150 and 200 m (492 and 656 ft) for technical divers. The saddle area is also a haven for bluespotted ribbontail rays, goatfish, pennantfish and yellowbar angelfish. Humphead (Napoleon) wrasse often follow divers around on this plateau, a throwback to when divers were allowed to feed them.

There is good but sparse coral growth on the outer walls but some wonderful patches of *Dendronephthya* soft tree corals on the eastern side of Jolanda Reef. In the strong currents the outer walls, particularly of Shark Reef, often have huge shoals of red snappers, unicornfish and trevallies as well as many pelagic species like barracuda and tuna. If you can stand the heat in summer, this site is spectacular from June to mid-August when the fish are spawning. In June I have also seen huge shoals of circular batfish. Unfortunately the ripping current here makes it very difficult to take pictures of these shoals with even the smallest housed camera. This is a place for photographers to use a Nikonos or small digital compact camera – even then the flash gun will be swept to one side.

Ideally divers should treat this dive as a drift-dive because of the currents and have their chase boat pick them up in the shallows beyond Jolanda Reef, this alleviates many of the current-related problems that are common here. Unfortunately, many of the day-boat skippers are lazy and also have snorkellers in the water so divers should be very careful to monitor their air consumption. For divers on a live-aboard boat, it is worth diving here before 8.00 am to get most of the dive over before the hordes of day-boats arrive. The currents are often weaker at this time.

Divers can swim a figure of eight around the two pinnacles, drift with the current or go backwards and forwards on the seaward side. The route divers take around the reef depends upon the current; either clockwise or counterclockwise. When they have finished their dive, they should be very careful on the ascent as the boat traffic can be very busy.

FACTS

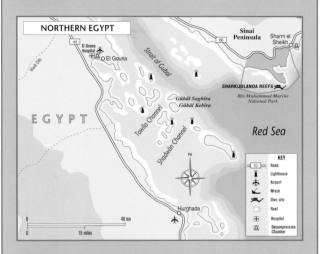

CLIMATE
Warm, mostly dry winters average 20ºC (68ºF), but cold and windy out to sea. Hot, dry summers average 35ºC (95ºF), but the winds at sea can be strong. Have warm clothes available if on a boat. Divers are only exposed to the heat ashore when travelling on land.

SEASONALITY
All year round but best April-August, it can be cold and rough in winter.

GETTING THERE
Fly to Sharm el Sheikh or to Cairo and then by road to Sharm el Sheikh, then either by road or by boat to Râs Muhammad.

WATER TEMPERATURE
Summers average 25ºC (77ºF), 19ºC (66ºF) in winter when a thick wetsuit or a dry-suit are preferable.

QUALITY OF MARINE LIFE
Very good, a high density of stony and soft corals, gorgonias, other invertebrates and both reef and pelagic fish including sharks.

DEPTH OF DIVES
Most places of interest are above 30 m (98 ft) but the depth is well beyond the accepted limits for sport divers on air.

SAFETY
Currents are strong and can be fierce.

WRECKS AND STRONG CURRENTS
EGYPT

Although the North Egyptian Red Sea is cheap and popular, apart from Shark and Jolanda Reef it is the offshore reefs of Southern Egypt that have the best diving.

Among these are the Brothers Islands (El Akhawein), Dædalus Reef (Abu El Kizan), Elphinstone Reef and Fury Shoal. Unique to Dædalus reef is a cave full of lionfish. Translated from Arabic, El Akhawein means 'The Two Brothers'. On a similar latitude to El Quseir on the Egyptian mainland, 52 km (32 miles) east of the western shore of the Egyptian Red Sea, The Brothers are two isolated seamounts rising as islands out of very deep water. Being part of the Offshore Marine Park Islands, only the fixed moorings can be used. The Brothers' steep walls take the full force of the prevailing currents and being the only real reefs in the area the currents produce upwellings full of nutrients that are a magnet for pelagic species as well as reef fish. They have wonderfully colourful *Dendronephthya* soft tree corals.

The Brothers are very exposed and therefore can only be reached in relatively calm seas. The crossing can be rough so use a heavy boat that is low in the water rather than a 'modern looking' vessel that is high in the water and likely to rock around excessively. Nowadays the Brothers are a live-aboard only destination and are best visited from May to July. The steep walls are not good for safe anchoring so in strong winds and currents the boat captain may not want to stay overnight.

Big Brother, less than a kilometre (0.6 miles) northwest of Little Brother, is much the larger of the two, oblong in shape and 400 m (1312 ft)-long. The drop-off is a wall descending to depths deeper than sport divers should dive, with gorgonian sea whips, sea fans and black corals in the deeper water and colourful soft corals in the shallow water. For most divers, the main attraction is the sharks – grey reef, scalloped hammerhead, silvertip, whitetip reef, thresher, oceanic whitetip and even tiger sharks. There are also large shoals of fish, especially in late spring and early summer when they gather to spawn. These include angelfish, butterflyfish, snappers, batfish, fusiliers, barracuda, halfbeaks, groupers, trevallies, surgeonfish (including unicornfish) and manta rays.

At Little Brother the currents have produced some of the most colourful *Dendronephthya* soft tree corals to be found in the Red Sea. The current runs east to west and on the southeast side there are superb gorgonian sea fans but the best are deep, starting at 35 m (115 ft), there are also plenty of caves, overhangs, black coral, and lots of pelagics including sharks, tuna, barracuda, turtles and shoals of reef fish. As divers swim round the southern corner, the slope gives way to a vertical wall. In summer thresher sharks are seen here, in October grey reef sharks gather to mate and divers have also seen shoaling scalloped hammerheads and occasionally sailfish.

Big Brother has two wrecks at its northern end. The large British freighter SS *Numidia*, which sank in 1901, now lies very steeply down the northernmost tip starting at 9 m (30 ft) with the stern at 80 m (262 ft). 100 m (328 ft)-south of the *Numidia*, the SS *Aïda* sank in 1957. The bow section is unrecognisable but the stern lies from 30-65 m (98-213 ft) and the rest of the vessel is scattered over the reef.

Although the *Numidia* lies at a seemingly impossible angle and plunges into technical diving depths this is a most beautiful wreck due to the abundance of soft corals. Ideally divers should aim for the areas of

Right A lionfish roams the wreck of the SS *Numidia*
Overpage A diver inspects coral growth on the SS *Aïda* wreck

weakest current but some current is required to show the Dendronephthya soft tree corals at their best. Divers can shelter from the currents within the superstructure. Visitors have not been able to take many artefacts so the outline of the metal parts of the ship is still well-marked, the lifeboat davits and winches are all still in place and the resident marine life includes big groupers. Some of the coral-encrusted rolling stock, the signature image of the *Numidia*, disappeared in the summer of 2006.

The 1,428 gross tonnes, 75 m (246 ft)-long, 9.7 m (32 ft)-beam SS *Aïda* was built in France in 1911. On September 15th, 1957 she struck rocks off Big Brother Island in a storm and began to sink. She now lies bow up, stern down, steeply down the wall at the northwest corner, the bow is at 30 m (98 ft) and the stern is at around 70 m (230 ft).

The two wrecks are too large to cover properly in a single dive.

Left A Dendronephtya soft coral colony expanded in the current, The Brothers

FACTS

CLIMATE
Hot and humid on land in summer but the winds at sea can be strong, thin wet suits are fine but it is wise to have warm clothes on the boat. Divers are only exposed to the heat ashore when travelling.

SEASONALITY
Best dived from May to July, charters run in other months but the sea can be rough.

GETTING THERE
There are two possible routes depending on your live-aboard's departure port – Hurghada/Port Safâga or Marsa 'Alam/Port Ghalib. For Hurghada/Port Safâga there are charter flights or connecting flights via Cairo to Hurghada airport, which is midway between Hurghada and Port Safâga. Then there is an asphalt road if you are heading for Marsa 'Alam and Port Ghalib. Charter flights or connecting flights via Cairo now go to Marsa 'Alam airport for Marsa 'Alam/Port Ghalib.

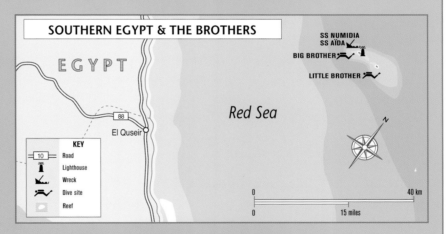

SOUTHERN EGYPT & THE BROTHERS

EGYPT

SS NUMIDIA
SS AÏDA
BIG BROTHER
LITTLE BROTHER

Red Sea

88

El Quseir

KEY
10 — Road
Lighthouse
Wreck
Dive site
Reef

0   40 km
0   15 miles

WATER TEMPERATURE
Average 27°C (81°F) in summer.

QUALITY OF MARINE LIFE
Very good, with a high density of stony and soft corals, gorgonias, other invertebrates and both reef and pelagic fish including sharks.

DEPTH OF DIVES
From the surface to depths well beyond the accepted limits of sport diving.

SAFETY
Currents are strong and can be fierce.

CONSHELF II
SUDAN

Sudanese waters from Port Sudan north to Angarosh have the best diving and largest species diversity in all of the Red Sea.

Sudan was one of the first countries to ban spear fishing and there are so many reefs that come up to the surface that large-scale commercial fishing has never been practical except for prawns in the sandy areas south of Port Sudan. Four of Sudan's dive sites are among the world's best: the South Point of Sha'b Rumi, the North and Southwest Points of Sanganeb and the *Umbria* Wreck.

There are numerous reefs in this area that are of interest to divers but it is the reefs near to Marsa 'Arus (Arous) and Port Sudan that are most popular.

East of Marsa 'Arus, 40 km (25 miles)-north-northeast of Port Sudan, Sha'b (Sha'ab) Rumi, which translates as Roman Reef, is a large, long reef with its longest sides parallel to the prevailing north to south current.

The site of Jacques-Yves Cousteau's Conshelf II underwater living experiment of 1963 is beside the reef, just outside of the lagoon on its west side, some 50 m (164 ft)-south of the southern of the two entrances to the lagoon. This blasted lagoon entrance is 10 m (33 ft)-wide and there is safe anchorage for small vessels inside the lagoon.

From the boat, the largest of the remains is just a large dark shadow, but once underwater, divers are faced with a scene more reminiscent of a science fiction film-set than their normal diving environment. The main object is a large, futuristic, onion-shaped steel structure standing on three legs and strewn with soft corals. This strange object is the saucer hangar.

Descending to 9 m (30 ft) and finning between the

three legs, lionfish flit away as divers squeeze up through the entrance hatch of the hanger. The portholes have gone, but above their empty sockets the structure is still gastight and filled with the exhaled gases of previous divers. A shoal of sweepers sheltering inside parts in panic and divers' bubbles distort reflections at the interface of the water and the trapped pocket of gases. Other fish hide in the space between the double-skin, which was used to position the lead ballast.

Except for coral growth, little has changed. As late as 1992 there was a prolific growth of Acropora table corals on the outside of the hangar, some over 1 m (39 inches)-across, but these have now broken away and the structure is festooned in soft corals. The wooden floor of the hangar has rotted away.

To the north, up current, is the tool shed. This is just a low shed with a corrugated roof, but as with the hangar it is notable for its coral growth. Beyond the tool shed the sand and a 3 m (10 ft)-high coral barrier are strewn with iron grids and massive steel hawsers, the cables that ran across the reef edge to the utility ship *Rosaldo* that was moored in the lagoon.

Beyond this, abreast of the lagoon entrance, are the strange multi-angular shapes and colours of the three metal and Perspex fish pens that are covered in Dendronephthya soft tree corals. These fish pens move around in rough seas and two of them have now collapsed but one is still reasonably intact. Steel hawsers and grids litter the site and together with a shark cage are all that remains below the drop-off, where the Deep Cabin was situated at 27 m (89 ft).

The site is full of nostalgia and by marking the lagoon entrance with a flashing light, makes an excellent night

Right A diver over one of the fish pens left over from the Conshelf II experiment

INDIAN OCEAN

CONSHELF TIMESCALE

In the early 1960's, Captain Jacques-Yves Cousteau wanted to demonstrate that humans could live and work on the ocean floor – more specifically, on the continental shelf, a submerged strip of land that extends from the edge of all the continents to depths of some 200 m (656 ft).

Three expeditions, known as Conshelf Stations I, II and III, were designed to compete for public attention with the large government-financed space programmes, divers living and working under pressure for long periods and the use of mixed gases, all of which we now take for granted.

Cousteau began with the Continental Shelf station number one (Conshelf I) in September 1962 off the island of Pomègues near Marseilles. Here Albert Falco and Claude Wesly spent seven days at 9 m (30 ft) in a cylindrical habitat 5 m (16 ft)-long and 2.5 m (8 ft)-wide.

The more ambitious Conshelf II was mainly sponsored by the French National Petroleum Office (Bureau de Recherches de Petròle), who had an obvious requirement for research into undersea petroleum production but to make ends meet Cousteau signed a contract to produce a full-length documentary film about the expedition.

To select a suitable site Albert Falco spent a month searching along a 130 km (81 mile) section of Red Sea reefs near Port Sudan and eventually settled on Sha'b Rumi (Sha'ab Rumi, 40 km (25 mile) northeast of Port Sudan. On its sheltered western side, Sha'b Rumi combined a reasonably level ledge at 9 m (30 ft) for the main station, with a steep drop-off nearby for the deep habitat. The lagoon gave safe anchorage for the utility ship *Rosaldo* and the reef was a reasonable distance from Port Sudan for the supply ship Calypso.

The four structures of the undersea 'village', were prefabricated in Nice by the Perona steel works and taken out to Port Sudan on the *Rosaldo*, where they were put together, ballasted and towed out to Sha'b Rumi. Three of the submersible buildings, the main habitat, the saucer hangar and the deep habitat, were designed to stand on telescopic legs so that they could be adjusted to be level. Their exit hatches were at the lowest points, open to the water and shark cages protected those on the two habitats.

Conshelf II covered the operation and maintenance of a scientific submersible, the 'saucer', from the underwater hangar, where it would be independent of the problems of launching from a pitching ship in rough seas. If such a station could operate in a remote area, then similar stations could be operated almost anywhere in the world. The saucer hangar had a drop-open floor, so that the saucer could enter from below. The water would then be pumped out by air pressure and the saucer could be worked on and the batteries charged in situ.

Sinking the underwater village was not easy, as the steady half-knot current made things tricky. The deep habitat sank several times before it was finally placed securely. The ballast racks for Starfish House held 80 tonnes (79 tons) of lead pigs, but a further 20 tonnes (20 tons) were necessary and extra racks for this had to be built. While lowering the saucer hangar, one of its legs gave way. The hangar tilted over and then all three legs collapsed. Only the much lighter tool shed and fish pens were easy to position. In all, some 200 tonnes (197 tons) of lead ballast were required.

Adjacent to the saucer hangar at 9 m (30 ft) there was a large and spacious long-stay habitat named Starfish House because it had four radiating arms. The short-stay Deep Cabin habitat was over the drop-off at 27 m (89 ft). This was a large upright cylinder with three levels, the upper two of which were living quarters and the one below, the diving centre.

When all was complete, the utility ship *Rosaldo* was moored in the safety of the lagoon, supplying compressed air, electricity, telephone communications and food, across a gantry built over the reef. Originally planned for March the experiment finally got underway in July 1963. Five men, Professor Raymond Vaissière, chief of the biological division of the Oceanographic Museum at Monaco, who was scientific director of both Conshelf I and II, Claude Wesly, André Folco,

Pierre Vannoni and the chef Pierre Guilbert, spent a month around and in the main Starfish House, breathing air at two atmospheres pressure. They used the old miners' trick of keeping a parrot in the habitat to give them early warning of any dangerous build up of carbon dioxide gas.

In the Deep Cabin Andre Portelatin and Raymond Kientzy spent a week at 27 m (89 ft), breathing a mixture of air and helium at 3.5 atmospheres, with working dives to 50 m (164 ft) and one short dive to 110 m (361 ft). This habitat had several problems including leaks, breaking cables and a tendency to slide off the steep slope on which it was moored while the divers were inside.

The hydrojet submarine *La Soucoupe Plongeante*, the diving saucer or DS2, was so named because it resembled a flying saucer. It was two metres (79 inches) in diameter and 1.5 m (59 inches)-high. Battery-powered, it had an oxygen rebreather system which could supply the crew for 24 hours.

For Conshelf III in 1965, Cousteau returned to the Mediterranean, off Cap-Ferrat. The habitat was a large two-storey sphere, which rested on a barge containing the ballast for raising and lowering the whole system. The upper level was for dining, communications and data gathering while the lower level contained the sleeping, sanitation and diving areas. This experiment was unique in that an oil well 'Christmas tree' was lowered near to the habitat so that the divers could test actual practical techniques. Six divers, including Cousteau's son Philippe, spent three weeks at 100 m (328 ft) breathing a mixture of oxygen and helium.

Below Conshelf II's underwater saucer hanger is now festooned with Dendronephthya soft tree corals

dive. Sharks are rare, except deep over the drop-off, but turtles and bottlenose dolphins are common.

The best time to dive the site is very early in the morning, after a quiet night. Then the sand will have settled and the visibility will be 30 m (98 ft) plus. A north-south current gets up every day, rising to around one knot in mid-afternoon. The site sees plenty of divers and even more snorkellers, from passing round-the-world yachties who use the safe anchorage in the lagoon. The stony coral outer wall, north along the outside of the lagoon, has some of the finest Dendronephthya soft tree corals to be found in the Red Sea.

The story of Conshelf II was recounted in the film *World Without Sun*. When the experiment was finished, the two habitats with their scientific equipment and the lead pigs were recovered, but what remains for today's divers to visit evokes memories of early underwater pioneers.

Left There is plenty of room for divers inside the Conshelf II saucer hanger

FACTS

CLIMATE
Winters are warm and dry but offshore winds can be very strong so have warm clothes on the boat at sea. Summers can reach 47°C (117°F) on land. On a live-aboard, you are only exposed to the heat when travelling on land. At sea the temperature is comfortable but humid. Thin wet suits are best in winter and Lycra Skins fine in summer.

SEASONALITY
Diving is possible all year but most live-aboard boats operating out of Port Sudan do so only in winter, though it can get very windy and rough at that time. Best times are May–July and September. Avoid August as heavy rains in nearby Ethiopia cause generally poor weather and south winds called *Haboobs*, which bring large amounts of dust and sand.

GETTING THERE
Fly to Port Sudan and then board a live-aboard boat to sail north. While it is possible to reach the site in small boats from nearby 'Arus it is not recommended.

WATER TEMPERATURE
Averages 28°C (82°F) in summer, 27°C (81°F) in winter. There can be highs of 30°C (86°F) in places; surface patches beside reefs can be hot.

QUALITY OF MARINE LIFE
The greatest density and diversity of reef and pelagic species in the Red Sea, especially sharks, is off Sudan – thanks to the absence of large-scale commercial fishing.

DEPTH OF DIVES
From the surface to depths well beyond the accepted limits of sport or recreational technical diving but the deepest point of the Conshelf site is 27 m (89 ft).

SAFETY
Very safe if divers remain above 10 m (33 ft) on the Conshelf site.

NIGHT DIVING
SUDAN

Many divers are addicted to night diving. There is so much to be seen that divers finish the dive bubbling with enthusiasm.

So long as there is not a strong current, almost anywhere will produce a good night dive, but it is even better if there is an easy entry and exit and easy navigation.

26 km (16 miles) northeast of Port Sudan, the deep-water jetty at the south end of Sanganeb Reef is one of the world's best night dives, combining ease of entry and exit with easy navigation along the face and being over 70-90 m (230-295 ft)-deep water means that there are even more species than usual to be encountered.

Divers may feel a touch of apprehension before jumping into water where, just a few hours earlier, they had been photographing sharks. Almost inevitably they first point the dive light into open water to confirm that there are no sharks around, but as they descend, there is so much life and colour lit up on the reef, that all such fears are forgotten.

Having fixed a flashing light at the point of entry so that they can easily find it to exit again, the divers go out against the current at 9–10 m (30–33ft).

Every nook and cranny in the coral contains something of interest, shrimps, prawns, crabs, lobsters,

Right Male bicolour parrotfish sleeping on feeding *tubastrea* corals at night, Sanganeb South Face

STONEFISH AND SCORPIONFISH

The well-camouflaged stonefish and scorpionfish feature high on the list of divers' worst nightmares but they are actually very common so the fact that few divers have trouble with them should help to put their minds at rest.

Thought to be the world's most venomous fish, stonefish spines contain toxic venom that can kill a child or a highly allergic adult, however most healthy adults only suffer extreme pain. Stonefish are found on the top of reefs or on the sand so the people most at risk are local fishermen who tread on them while walking over the reef collecting shellfish.

True stonefish remain still in a horizontal position for very long periods of time such that depending on the habitat they either allow algae to grow on their body or sand to cover it for further camouflage. They are generally green, red-brown or grey/sandy coloured and are usually only seen if they move. Flatter than scorpionfish, their eyes usually face almost straight up and the mouth is hardly discernible among the camouflage.

The less toxic and more easily seen scorpionfish have a more fishlike, upright body shape and their eyes face sideways rather than upward, the mouth is usually obvious. They lie all over reefs in any position depending on the shape of the substrata. They do not rely on additional camouflage but change their body colour to match the substrate. The most common colour is dark red but they can change through red and red-brown to white. Their greatest risk to divers is at night where they are rarely visible outside of the narrow beam of the dive-light. At night they are usually coloured red so they are easily spotted against coral if directly lit up but there are also many small juveniles about, which are usually buried in the coral during the day.

Again, those most at risk are local fishermen clearing their nets by hand. I have treated several local fishermen who had either trodden on stonefish spines or caught their hands on scorpionfish spines or lionfish, all complained of extreme pain but all survived to do it again. Antivenin is rarely available and requires refrigeration, immersion of the wounded limb in hot water at 50°C (120°F) until the pain stops is now the recommended treatment.

THE CORAL REEF AT NIGHT

Night on a coral reef is a time of change; dusk and dawn are the times of most predator activity and these animals can rise unseen out of the darkness to take prey made visible against the lighter sky above.

Divers can often sit on a boat or jetty watching the water churn as shoals of small fish are attacked by trevallies, tuna or barracuda. Often these small fish jump out of the water in an attempt to escape, only to be snapped up by hovering sea birds.

Underwater, parrotfish and butterflyfish hide in crevices in the reef, angelfish penetrate even further, either completely hidden or with just an eye or snout to be seen. Many wrasse bury themselves in the sand together with some pufferfish, lizardfish, flounders and rays – not a foolproof strategy as many sharks have electroreceptors that can detect them and dolphins can echolocate fish under the sand. Snappers and grunts shoal in closely knit small groups, in caves, in small valleys or between gorgonias.

Triggerfish flatten themselves against depressions in the coral, as do the smaller hawksbill and green turtles if they cannot find a cave or large enough gorgonian.

Many diurnal fish change colour at night. Sometimes this change is small but in other cases there is a total change, and occasionally the colour change is similar to that used by the same fish at a cleaning station to signal that it is ready for cleaning. In some instances solid colours become blotchy in others bold patterns appear making the fish more difficult to pick out against the background.

TIPS ON NIGHT DIVING

1. Choose an area with the least wave and current action and easy marks for navigation.
2. Dive the area during daylight first to familiarize yourself with the topography.
3. The easiest night dives for navigation are along reef edges.
4. If there is a current, go out against it and back with it.
5. If you are new to night diving, begin with a dusk dive.
6. Wear protective clothing, as you are certain to bump into things.
7. Check that all diving and camera equipment is functioning correctly before you enter the water, then check again when you are in the water.
8. Avoid lights that are too bright and carry a spare as a backup – underwater lights are notorious for failing. Remember that rechargeable torches go out suddenly without warning. Use alkaline batteries in your backup light. Small waterproof torches make good, cheap, back-up lights and can be used as focusing lights by photographers. Use a lanyard between your dive light and your wrist.
9. If you wish to gain another diver's attention it is important to point your dive light down onto your hand with a circular motion so as not to blind the other divers.
10. Helmet or head-mounted torches are a nuisance due to back scatter from plankton and other small creatures.
11. Avoid dangling equipment that will snag.
12. If you are beach diving, align two lights on shore in the direction of your exit.
13. If you are boat diving, fix chemical light sticks or a flashing light to the boarding ladder and ascent/descent line.
14. If you use a chemical light stick, make sure that you retrieve it and dispose of it properly.
15. Set a turnaround time, e.g. 30-minutes out and 30-minutes back.
16. Do not try to cover large distances. Take your time and look closely in nooks and crannies for small creatures.
17. Have warm dry clothing and a hot drink ready for when return.

Left A manta ray is attracted by divers' lights during a night dive

cuttlefish, worms and octopuses. Nudibranchs, urchins, flat worms, cowrie shells, tun shells and conch shells graze the coral. Overhanging roofs become a blaze of colour from the feeding polyps of Tubastrea corals.

A sea hare grazes sedately and ejects magenta ink if disturbed. A moray eel dashes from crevice to crevice; a clownfish looks forlorn, shut out of its closed anemone. Comb jellies, often too transparent to be noticed in daylight, stand out in the divers' lights.

Young cuttlefish and shellfish hide among the long spines of spiny urchins and small crabs feed among the arms of brittle stars and gorgonias. The shallows are the realm of basket stars, brittle stars and feather stars, sifting the current for plankton. If the divers' lights are too powerful, the animals will curl up and disappear more quickly than the divers can look at them, so it is best to use a weak light.

The daytime reef fish hide in holes in the reef or behave sleepily on top of it. They are often mesmerized by the dive lights and thus easily photographed. Most interesting are the larger parrotfish, which back into unlikely looking overhangs, holes or branched corals and have apparently gone to sleep: their eyes are still open, but they ignore the lights. By diving late, divers find them enclosed in a cocoon of mucous, which is believed to protect them from predators and parasites. Many fish will spread out their fins to appear larger and more threatening, and some pufferfish will inflate for the same reason.

The dangers of night diving are not sharks, which are rarely seen at night; while divers vision is limited to the range and width of the beam of the dive lights, it is easy for them to brush against unseen objects such as fire coral, lionfish, stinging hydroids, spiny

Below When taken by surprise, porcupine pufferfish act as though a predator is after them and inflate their bodies so as to be larger

urchins, scorpion fish and stonefish. A scorpionfish goes bright red in a beam of light, so it is easily seen. It is surprising to see just how many scorpionfish there are at night, including many young that go unseen during the day. Stonefish are more difficult to see at night and often only give themselves away by their movement.

Sanganeb has Spanish dancers, bright red nudibranchs fringed with white, which grow up to 20 cm (8 inches)-long. There are plenty of them about but they are often hard to pick out, as they blend in with the red sponges. The divers turn around after 30-minutes and follow the current back at 3-5 m (10-16 ft).

Before finishing the dive, the divers switch off their dive lights for a few minutes; initially they are surprised by all the cracking noises of the various creatures eating and snapping. As their eyes get used to the dark, they see many phosphorescent creatures, including flashlight fish (*Photoblepharon*), who swim around in small shoals. A pouch below each of their eyes contains millions of luminescent bacteria, which glow like fireflies. As the divers move about they also disturb millions of phosphorescent plankton.

There is nothing to be gained by going deep on a night dive – 9–10 m (30–33 ft) is deep enough to see everything, and considering that the divers have probably already made two dives during the day, a third dive could cause dangerous recompression problems if they go any deeper.

If you have never been on a night dive, it's an experience not to be missed. Even night snorkelling with torches along the reef edge can be very rewarding. It's a new and different underwater world, with some strange creatures to be seen.

FACTS

CLIMATE
Hot and humid on land in summer, but the winds at sea can be strong, thin wet suits are fine but it is wise to have warm clothes on the boat.

SEASONALITY
All year round except when there are southerly winds in August, these can produce *Haboobs* (sandstorms) and rough weather on south-facing dives.

GETTING THERE
There are international air connections to Port Sudan, then by boat 26 km (16 miles) northeast to the deepwater jetty at the south end of Sanganeb Reef.

WATER TEMPERATURE
Averages 28°C (82°F) in summer, 27°C (81°F) in winter.

QUALITY OF MARINE LIFE
Very good, with a high density of stony and soft corals, gorgonias, other invertebrates and both reef and pelagic fish including Sharks.

DEPTH OF DIVES
From the surface to 9–10 m (30–33 ft). The bottom is well beyond the accepted limits of sport diving.

SAFETY
There is normally a gentle current along the reef but the dive can be impossible when there are southerly winds in August.

SARDINE AND SQUID RUNS
SOUTH AFRICA

South Africa's coast faces the Atlantic and Indian Oceans and the 20-degree meridian east of Greenwich through Cape Agulhas denotes their separation point.

South Africa is famous for cage diving with great white sharks in the Atlantic Ocean but until recently only local divers were found along the Indian Ocean coast, which runs from the Eastern Cape to the Mozambican border. However, nowadays local operators are enticing international divers with trips covering exciting aggregations of squid and sardines and their predators.

THE CHOKKA SQUID RUN

Squid, also known as Calamari, the plural form of the Italian word for squid, Calamaro, is known as 'white gold' to fishermen because of its value. The most abundant squid in southern African waters, chokka (*Loligo vulgaris reynaudii*) is found all along the southern Cape Coast and during the summer months they become concentrated in inshore areas of the Eastern Cape, particularly in the bays between Cape Point and Port Elizabeth.

Chokka spawn throughout the year but the peak time is October to December, when to protect the spawning stock the chokka fishing industry observes an annual closed season for a month. This is the time when divers can best observe this amazing event.

Although the mating itself is interesting, it is the hundreds of predators that quickly appear to feast on the squid and their eggs that makes the event thrilling. The feeding frenzy attracts cape fur seals, Copper (bronze whaler) and raggedtooth sharks, common, and Indian Ocean bottlenose dolphins, various small sharks, large rays, common octopuses and a range of predatory fishes and birds.

A good area to dive with the squid is out of Port St Francis, the biggest chokka fishing port in South Africa, which is in St Francis Bay, 120 km (75 miles) west of Port Elizabeth.

The squid mate in the water column above the seabed and spawn predominantly on a sandy bottom. The resulting pale orange egg clusters waving about in the surge may cover large areas and the thousands of squid moving from their mating depth to the egg beds make a spectacular sight.

The translucent squid lay their eggs and then try to defend them from an onslaught of predators. Rays or sharks swimming over the egg beds may cause minimal disturbance to the egg laying activity, but a seal swooping down on the beds will clear the area of squid for at least a minute.

Local operators find the aggregations of squid with their electronic fish-finders though the action of predators on the surface tends to give the site's position away. The action is fast and unpredictable, the water clarity is often poor and there is no guarantee that the spawning will start on a given date. However each event is relatively static so once divers find an egg cluster they can wait for the predatory action to begin.

There is no fixed dive site and the depth can be anything from 10-50 m (33-164 ft). Due to the seasonality, dive operators tend to be mobile.

THE SARDINE RUN

The annual migration northwards of South African/South American pilchard (*Sardinops sagax*) from the cold depths off Cape Agulhas to KwaZulu-

Right A copper shark and South African fur seal in pursuit of sardines

INDIAN OCEAN

Natal from May to July every year offers an amazing spectacle. The only member of the genus *Sardinops* found in the Indo-Pacific, the fish reach a length of up to 40 cm (16 inches).

The sardines form vast shoals off the Agulhas Banks and as the southerly Agulhas current weakens they move north in shoals that have been recorded up at to 15 km (9.5 miles)-long, 3 km (2 miles)-wide and up to 40 m (130 ft)-deep. Experts are still not sure why the fish leave nutrient-rich feeding grounds for emptier, sub-tropical climes but thermal satellite images suggest that cool water coming up the coast

Below Long-beaked common dolphins prey on a baitball of sardines

in the winter months allows them to extend their range, and as soon as their food source runs out they turn back. In winters when there is warm water close to shore, the Agulhas current remains too strong and there is either no sardine run, or it is limited to the area around Port Elizabeth.

The sardines travel close to the shore and are followed by hundreds of predators that are responsible for causing some fish to break away from the main shoal in what is known as a bait ball and this results in a feeding frenzy as sardines dart in all directions trying to escape from hundreds of underwater predators.

The diversity of predators feasting on the sardines as they migrate includes cape fur seals, copper, raggedtooth, dusky and blacktip sharks, common and Indian Ocean bottlenose dolphins, orcas, bryde's whales, a variety of larger predatory fishes including game fishes and several species of birds. Supported by

spotter-planes, dive operators do their best to locate the sardines for divers.

The timing cannot be guaranteed and the event may not happen every year. As the distance covered is large and the terrain of the coastline is wide ranging there are variations in visibility and in some areas the sardines come right inshore, even up to the beach. The type of predator, sea conditions and diving facilities vary along different sections of the coastline. Launches through surf can also be tricky. Divers and snorkellers should be very careful around bait balls as it is easy to get bitten in error by larger predators.

The action is over in about 20 minutes because the bait ball becomes too small so divers return to the boat to search for another one.

Divers and snorkellers are dependent on the local operator and the pilots of spotter planes to find the bait balls. The dives are surface drifts in open water but there is no need to go below 20 m (66 ft).

FACTS

CLIMATE
Usually mild 17–21°C (63–70°F).

SEASONALITY
Chokka spawning: October to December.
Sardine Run: May to July.

GETTING THERE
There are International air links to Cape Town, then on by road.

WATER TEMPERATURE
Chokka Spawning: 8-22°C (46-72°F)
Sardine Run: Usually 15–17°C (60–63°F)

QUALITY OF MARINE LIFE
A high density of the larger predators including sharks.

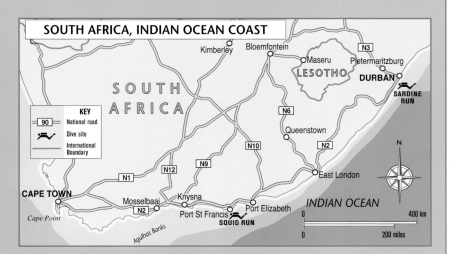

SOUTH AFRICA, INDIAN OCEAN COAST

DEPTH OF DIVES
Near to or on the surface, rarely below 40 m (131 ft).

SAFETY
Currents can be strong.

MANTA RAYS
THE MALDIVES

Situated off the southern tip of India, about 700 km (435 miles) southwest of Sri Lanka with a few minor atolls just south of the equator, the Republic of the Maldives is an archipelago of 26 major atolls containing over 1,190 coral reef islands.

The Maldives has myriad of diving and snorkelling sites and with the development of areas that were previously off-limits, new dive sites are being located in atolls ranging from Huvadhoo in the south to Haa Alifu in the North.

The wide variety of dive sites in the Maldives makes it suitable for divers of all levels of experience. Each atoll has sheltered reefs in lagoons suitable for novices, and channels between the atoll's lagoon and the open ocean where fast-flowing currents flowing in and out with the tides produce top drift-diving for experienced divers.

The monsoon weather gives two distinct seasons in the Maldives. In the Maldivian summer the northeast monsoon from December to April has drier conditions and currents that flow from the northeast to southwest. Visibility on the eastern sides of the atolls is good. The currents are usually stronger at the start of the season and decrease in strength as the season progresses. From February the waters calm down and through March to April there is easy diving and slacker currents. Visibility is worse on the western sides of the atolls because plankton and debris are washed out of the lagoons into the ocean, but because of this divers are likely to encounter large plankton feeders such as manta rays and whale sharks.

In the southwest monsoon from May to December there is good diving on the western sides of the atolls but manta rays and whale sharks will mainly be found off the eastern edge of the atolls.

The Maldives are unique in the Indian Ocean in that they host a year round population of whale sharks. Recent observations show that almost all of these animals are juvenile males less than 9 m (30 ft)-long. Some of the whale sharks are known to move between South Ari Atoll and South Maalhosmadulu Atoll (Baa) at different times of the year. Eventually they leave the atolls and disappear into the unknown.

South Ari Atoll is on the western edge of the Maldives and the nearest landfall to the west is Somalia in Africa. It is thought that the currents crossing this large expanse of water cause nutrient-rich uprisings that add to the plankton from the lagoons that attract large filter feeders.

The Maldives also have a large population of resident manta rays that migrate across the atolls with the changing monsoons as they follow the seasonal shift of their planktonic food. Manta cleaning stations require a strong current that enables the mantas to remain stationary for cleaning while still passing fresh oxygenated water through their gills. Such sites are usually found in the shallows on the top of submerged reefs rising to within 8-12 m (26-39 ft) of the surface where the likely cleaner fish are abundant. Recent studies suggest a larger number of adult females compared with males at Maldives cleaning stations.

Although the tourist resorts have good house reefs and may offer day-boat diving, serious divers are better off using live-aboard boats as these give access to a wider range of sites and get to the best sites early in the day to see the maximum amount fish life. There are more than 700 species of fish, 60 species of coral and a huge number of invertebrates.

Right A majestic manta ray soars overhead

INDIAN OCEAN

RASFARI

A spectacular ocean reef off the west side of the northern part of Malé Atoll, Rasfari is a protected marine area just outside of the uninhabited island of Rasfari. Exposed to south and northwesterly winds, it is sheltered during the northeast monsoon season. Cutting across a wide outside reef divers can find many sandy inlets and ridges. The reef slopes and falls down to a plateau at 20-30 m (66-98 ft), then drops down to 40 m (131 ft) and more. A circular thila, an isolated flat topped reef rising sharply from the inner atoll floor, with its top at 25-28 m (82-92 ft) is found on the plateau about 70 m (230 ft) out. This thila may be difficult to reach if the current is flowing against the divers.

The currents around the thila can be strong but as many as 12 manta rays have been seen plus grey reef, whitetip reef sharks, spotted eagle rays, giant reef rays, bigeye trevallies, parrotfish, great barracuda, fusiliers, bluestriped snappers and surgeonfish, especially on the edge of the thila intercepting the current. At the corner of Rasfari Kandu the currents can increase rapidly so divers should take care of outgoing currents that push them away from the reef.

Left At cleaning stations, manta rays will ignore divers if they remain quiet

FACTS

CLIMATE
Tropical, warm and humid. The Maldives have a complex weather pattern: a drier northeast monsoon season and wetter southwest monsoon season. The temperature is 24–30°C (75–86°F).

SEASONALITY
There is good diving all year but the northeast monsoon season, from December to April, is the most settled time. Divers have to be aware of the differences between the two monsoon seasons. There is not any river runoff so rainfall does not affect the visibility. May is the wettest month.

GETTING THERE
Flights to Malé international airport on Hulhulé Island, 2.5 km (1.5 miles) northeast of Malé, then onward by either boat or plane.

WATER TEMPERATURE
24–30°C (75–86°F).

QUALITY OF MARINE LIFE
Very good for corals and fauna including manta rays and whale sharks.

DEPTH OF DIVES
The best marine life is between 5 and 30 m (16 and 98 ft). Dives deeper than 30 m (98 ft) are prohibited.

SAFETY
Currents in the channels and outside of the atolls are often strong.

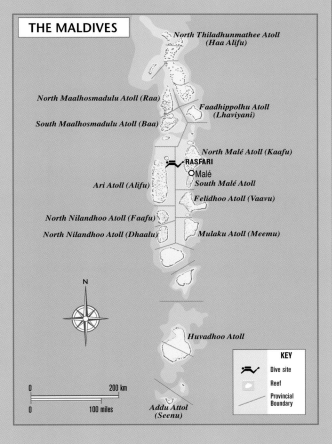

THE MALDIVES

North Thiladhunmathee Atoll (Haa Alifu)

North Maalhosmadulu Atoll (Raa)

Faadhippolhu Atoll (Lhaviyani)

South Maalhosmadulu Atoll (Baa)

North Malé Atoll (Kaafu)

RASFARI

Malé

Ari Atoll (Alifu)

South Malé Atoll

Felidhoo Atoll (Vaavu)

North Nilandhoo Atoll (Faafu)

North Nilandhoo Atoll (Dhaalu)

Mulaku Atoll (Meemu)

N

Huvadhoo Atoll

KEY

Dive site

Reef

Provincial Boundary

0   200 km

0   100 miles

Addu Attol (Seenu)

MANTA RAYS, THE MALDIVES

DIVING WITH SHARKS IN THE INDO-PACIFIC

Shallow reefs contain myriad of colourful sights and a cacophony of sounds, as their inhabitants feed and fight for territory, but in deeper water the colours fade to blue and the sounds to zero.

The silence heightens the senses as divers peer out into the ominous void. They expect sharks, and this thought plays on their minds. They may even be disappointed at only spotting sharks' hazy outlines on the limit of visibility.

The water may be blue, blue-grey or blue-green, depending on siltation, plankton and local mineral content. Whatever the colour, many predators have evolved countershading. Light coloration on their abdomen, which makes them difficult to discern against the surface from below, grey, grey-black or grey-brown coloration dorsally, making them almost invisible from above and gradual shading from dark to light on their sides allowing them to blend in with the mid-water background. At dusk or dawn, most sharks patrol shallow waters for food and are easily seen, but during the day they cruise in deeper water, where they are difficult to discern.

There are several reefs around the world where there are good places for viewing sharks. Many of these sites are where the points of reefs protrude into strong currents but have small sheltered areas where divers can observe the action. Currents of different velocities either mix forming whirlpools or collide with the reef but both form upwellings that bring rich nutrients that attract large shoals of fish and in turn sharks.

Blacktip reef sharks cruise in shallow water along the margins of reefs or beaches. Timid whitetip reef sharks scurry for the safety of caves and crevices and hammerhead sharks appear below or out in open water; but divers may get some shocks as grey reef and silvertip sharks suddenly rocket up out of the depths.

Grey reef sharks may be found resting on sand, which makes them visible, but otherwise divers are unlikely to know they are around until they suddenly appear out of the blue. Scalloped hammerhead sharks can be particularly frustrating. Divers spot them in shoals deep down, but if they descend to that level, they then find them swimming above! Scalloped hammerhead sharks appear to be harmless but mesmerizing,

their eyes lock on to divers and swivel in their sockets to keep them in view as they pass by.

Grey reef sharks often check divers out. In some regions the bolder ones drop their pectoral fins, arch their back and make stiff movements, although this is not a universal occurrence, if this does happen it is a warning that you are encroaching on their territory and it is wise to quietly return the way you came.

The first warning that silky sharks or tiger sharks are

around is often that other sharks disappear; they should be treated with caution, as they are generally troublesome.

Silvertip sharks tend to be in deeper water but will rise to shallow water to investigate a commotion or the scent of bait. They can be 3 m (10 ft)-long so they are some of the largest, most imposing sharks that divers are likely to encounter in warm water. Heavily built but streamlined in shape, they are almost black on top with a shiny skin and white tips to fins and tail. Spending most of the day in deep water, they do not arch their bodies, but just drop their pectoral fins and swim straight at you. They usually turn off at the last moment on the first approach, but further approaches may include nudging. Silvertip sharks are attracted by the whining of recharging strobes and together with grey reef sharks, silky sharks and some groupers, often mouth light coloured camera housings,

fins and kneepads in an exploratory way. All of these would appear to be a separate meal-sized morsel to the fish concerned. Silvertip sharks have been caught with 60 cm (23.5 inch) grey reef sharks in their stomachs. They are particularly persistent and should be treated with respect.

Sharks are more territorial in open water, where they have an unerring ability to appear behind you. As a general rule you should not hang around on the surface away from the reef. The usual reason for diving deep is to look for sharks. Without bait or speared fish in the water, there is little chance of serious trouble, but if you are harassed it is wise to calmly return to the boat. Where silvertips or silkies are common, your dive tender should remain on station, so that any divers that become worried can quickly leave the water. The only predictable thing about sharks is their unpredictability!

Below A diver encounters a grey reef shark

WHALE SHARKS
WESTERN AUSTRALIA

Following the synchronized mass coral spawning where sperm and eggs are released into the ocean at Ningaloo Reef in Western Australia around March or April each year, whale sharks migrate in numbers to this reef to feed on plankton, small fish or squid until June or July.

Ningaloo Marine Park is one of the world's most reliable locations to see whale sharks.

Located along the coast of Western Australia, Ningaloo Marine Park stretches 260 km (162 miles) southwards from Bundegi Reef in the Exmouth Gulf to Red Bluff just below the Tropic of Capricorn. The Park covers 5,076 sq km (1,960 sq miles) and includes both State Waters – those within the three-nautical-mile-limit, 2,640 sq km (1,019 sq miles) and Commonwealth Waters – those outside the three-nautical-mile-limit, 2,436 sq km (941 sq miles) – the waters and seabed of the continental shelf and slope which extend 5.6-17 km (3-9 nautical miles) seaward from the State boundaries. The reef ranges from 7 km (4.4 miles) to less than 200 m (656 ft) from the shore.

Named after an Aboriginal word for promontory, Ningaloo Reef surrounds the North West Cape and is both Australia's largest fringing reef and one of the world's largest fringing reefs. Its main feature is the rapid drop off in depth in the park's north where there are depths of 100 m (328 ft) within 6 km (3.7 miles) of the coast. This means that whale sharks and other pelagic fish are found unusually close to the shore.

Although best known for its whale sharks, Ningaloo is also rich in coral and other marine life. Dugongs feed on shallow sea grasses along the coast, manta rays are also attracted by the plankton and during the winter months the reef is part of the migratory routes for dolphins and humpback whales.

Off Ningaloo Reef, locating whale sharks in a wide expanse of open water depends on the skill of trained spotter aircraft pilots looking for the tell-tale signs of the sharks on the surface.

Right The massive tail of a whale shark at Ningaloo Reef

SNORKELLING WITH WHALE SHARKS

The largest cold-blooded animal and the largest fish in the world, the annual visit by whale sharks on migration is a major attraction for tourists at Ningaloo Reef and has become so popular that a Code-of-Conduct for interacting with whale sharks has been introduced to make sure that they are not harassed:

Boats: An exclusive contact zone of 250 m (820 ft)-radius applies to vessels around any whale shark and only one vessel at a time may operate within the zone for a maximum time of 90 minutes and at a speed of 15 km/hr (8 knots) or less. The vessel's tender approaching from ahead of the shark's direction of travel must remain over 30 m (98 ft) from the shark

Swimmers: People are not allowed to SCUBA dive with the whale sharks – only snorkelling is allowed. There is a maximum limit of 8 people allowed in the water at any one time. One must not attempt to touch a whale shark, restrict its movement or approach closer than 3 m (10 ft) from the head or body and 4 m (13 ft) from the tail and not swim in front of the animal's pectoral fins.

Photographers: Must not use flash (strobes).

The skippers of whale shark charter vessels are in radio contact with these pilots, who direct them to the sharks from the air.

There is great excitement at encountering a whale shark in the water, with its huge mouth open and entourage of remoras and pilot fish such as juvenile golden trevallies. This is hardly tempered by the strenuous effort of swimming strongly to keep up with the animal. To avoid irritating the shark and causing it to dive, snorkellers are instructed to minimize splashing, not to swim either in front of the pectoral fins or above the shark and to stay on the surface. Personal safety is particularly important, a whale shark may mean no harm, but its considerable bulk and giant tail is capable of inflicting serious damage to a person. Most snorkellers are able to stay alongside the whale shark for two to eight minutes before regrouping to be picked up by the boat.

The Ningaloo Reef charter operators are so confident they can find the whale sharks that they will take people on a second trip for free if they don't find one the first time.

While scientists believe that whale sharks reach 18 m (59 ft)-long, and fishermen regularly claim to have seen them longer, the Ningaloo Reef specimens are usually less than half of this size, sexually immature males with unused claspers. Throughout the world the largest whale shark that has been officially measured is 12.65 m (41 ft 6 in). Most whale sharks that are encountered by divers around the world are immature males. Every year the ones seen at Ningaloo Reef appear to be getting smaller, which is probably due to commercial fishing. The latest research suggests that some whale sharks encountered at Ningaloo Reef then migrate to feed on the mass release of eggs by red crabs at Christmas Island and then on to Indonesia before returning to Ningaloo Reef.

Left A diver videos a whale shark off Ningaloo Reef

Overpage Up close with a potato cod at Cod Hole, Great Barrier Reef

FACTS

CLIMATE
Hot summer (November to April) and temperate for the rest of the year with low rainfall. Temperatures range from 26-32°C (80-90°F). Seasonal tropical cyclones (predominantly in February and March) can have a devastating effect with high winds and strong wave action.

SEASONALITY
Best dived from April to June/July. Avoid the tropical cyclones that are predominantly in February and March.

GETTING THERE
Perth International Airport is serviced by many international carriers, and has a nearby domestic airport providing services to the northern coastal regions. Learmonth airport is 35 km (22 miles) south of Exmouth and 100 km (62 miles) from Coral Bay. The alternative is a scenic but slow road journey along the outback coastal highway. From Perth, Coral Bay is 1,132 km (703 miles) and Exmouth is 1,270 km (789 miles). Greyhound Australia and others offer regular bus departures.

WATER TEMPERATURE
22-30°C (72-86°F).

QUALITY OF MARINE LIFE
Very good for both corals and marine animals.

DEPTH OF DIVES
At the surface for whale sharks.

SAFETY
The snorkelling with whale sharks is in open water.

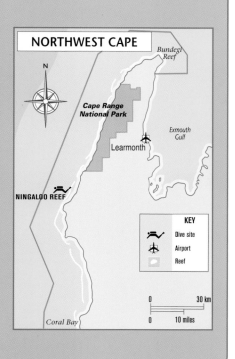

NORTHWEST CAPE

Bundegi Reef
N
Cape Range National Park
Exmouth Gulf
Learmonth
NINGALOO REEF

KEY
Dive site
Airport
Reef

0   30 km
0   10 miles

Coral Bay

WHALE SHARKS, WESTERN AUSTRALIA

TURTLES AND PRISTINE REEFS
MALAYSIA

Malaysia has always had good diving but it was the discovery of Pulau Sipadan that placed Malaysian diving in the world-class league with the world's best beach diving: there is a deep drop-off only a few swimming strokes from the beach on the west side of the jetty.

35 km (22 miles) south of Semporna, off the southeast coast of Sabah, the island lies just north of the equator in the Celebes (Sulawesi) Sea.

Malaysia's only volcanic island, Pulau Sipadan is perched on top of a volcanic seamount rising abruptly from 600 m (1,969 ft). Smaller than other diving destinations, it is only 12 ha (30 acres) in area, never rising more than a few metres above sea level. Covered in tropical rainforest and ringed with a narrow, white sand beach, one can walk around the perimeter beach in 15-20 minutes.

Pulau Sipadan translates as 'Border Island' in Malay because it lies on the border of Indonesia and Malaysia.

In 1989 Captain Jacques-Yves Cousteau and his team arrived in the research vessel *Calypso* and he was moved to say, "I have seen other places like Sipadan, 45 years ago, but now no more. Now we have found an untouched piece of art".

In the shallow water areas of Pulau Sipadan high coral cover is re-establishing itself after some bleaching. There are large areas of staghorn and table corals, plate and lettuce corals, boulder and brain corals, encrusting corals, bubble corals and solitary mushroom corals.

Interspersed among the stony corals are large leathery corals of the *Sarcophyton* and *Sinularia* species,

the constantly pulsating *Xenia* species, and colourful *Dendronephthya* soft tree corals. There are sponges, including vase and barrel sponges, sea squirts, oysters and giant clams.

The drop-off walls are less luxuriant, but have colourful *Tubastrea* and *Dendrophyllia* species under overhangs, together with sponges, Gorgonian sea fans and *Dendronephthya* soft tree corals. Deeper down the walls are larger Gorgonian sea fans, black corals and large barrel sponges covered in alabaster sea cucumbers.

Divers are regularly buzzed by shoals of fusiliers, barracuda, batfish, sweetlips, trevallies, goatfish and a huge shoal of bumphead parrotfish approaching 100 in number that can appear on any dive. There are several different varieties of clownfish.

Visibility is unpredictable – it can be murky one day and crystal-clear the next.

Right A turtle cruising over a healthy coral reef at Barracuda Point, Pulau Sipadan

Overpage The distinctive profile of a hawksbill turtle, Pulau Sipadan

PUFFERFISH TETRODOTOXIN

Pufferfish are extremely dangerous to eat, and they are responsible for some 30 deaths each year in Japan where the fish is eaten as a delicacy (where it is known as *fugu*). Pufferfish livers and ovaries contain Tetrodotoxin, an anaesthetic 160,000 times more potent than cocaine and 500 times stronger than cyanide.

Taken in tiny quantities however, the toxin cuts down cravings in the brain by calming signals in the hypothalamus, the section of the brain that coordinates the senses and controls feelings of addiction. This has led to it being incorporated into a drug, which is undergoing trials as a pain killer and as a replacement for Methadone in weaning drug addicts off their habit.

What makes Pulau Sipadan really stand out are the turtles. Massive green turtles and smaller hawksbill turtles are everywhere. Often 20-30 are seen on one dive, usually continuing with the serious business of eating, sleeping, mating or scratching parasites off their backs on the coral, while totally ignoring divers' close presence.

Turtles haul themselves laboriously up the beach to lay eggs after nightfall when the tide is high. They should never be disturbed before they start laying or they will give up and return to the sea: walking around the island at night without a ranger is now forbidden.

Pulau Sipadan soon attracted more divers than was sensible for the environment. Eventually numbers were restricted but now it is no longer possible to stay on the island overnight. Clients must either stay at Pulau Kapalai or Pulau Mabul, which are 15-minutes away by speedboat; some use a live-aboard boat, one of the resorts further away or the town of Semporna.

Below A large gorgonian sea fan at right angles to the prevailing current to feed, Pulau Sipadan

All boat dives are treated as drift dives, which cuts down on anchor damage.

Pulau Sipadan's currents are unpredictable. On some days Barracuda Point and South Point have ripping currents and on other days none. Several times a three knot current will suddenly totally reverse in direction.

Shore dives and night dives are best made from the beach on the west side of the jetty, where a swim of 5-10 m (16-33 feet), depending on the height of the tide, takes divers to the drop-off.

BARRACUDA POINT

This site is named after a very large shoal (500-1000) of barracuda that often used to be seen on the point. These barracuda move around – they are often seen at the South Point and sometimes disappear for weeks.

The site varies with depth, but the shallower waters consists of coral heads on coral rubble and sand, sloping gently out and down. At the point itself there are garden eels, many whitetip reef sharks and the occasional zebra (leopard) shark lying on the sand during the day, but they are very timid and difficult to approach closely. Lone hammerhead sharks are seen regularly and whale sharks occasionally.

At sand level there are blue and yellow sea squirts, nudibranchs, flat worms, bluespotted ribbontail rays, giant moray eels, cuttlefish, many varieties of pufferfish, scorpionfish and leaf scorpionfish, stonefish, surgeonfish, flounders, crocodilefish, various sponges and anemones with clownfish.

In open water there are spotted and Vlaming's unicornfish, moorish idols, Picasso, orangestriped and clown triggerfish. Trumpetfish hide in whip corals, colourful feather stars spread out in the current on any raised support they can find and various pelagic species cruise around.

Longnose hawkfish hide in Gorgonian sea fans, coral trout soldierfish and Zaizer's bigeyes in cracks in the coral and humphead (Napoleon) wrasse and golden rabbitfish cruise around.

The average depth is 14 m (46 ft) and the maximum depth is well beyond the depth at which sport divers can dive.

FACTS

CLIMATE
Climate: 26–30ºC (80–86ºF), tropical, warm and humid all year and rarely below 20ºC (68ºF).

SEASONALITY
The islands around Pulau Sipadan can be dived year-round but the weather is best May–October. August is the high season for both local holidays and turtle nesting.

GETTING THERE
To visit the islands around Pulau Sipadan fly to Kota Kinabalu, then take a domestic flight to Tawau. Then go by road to Semporna. Divers can visit Pulau Sipadan by boat or live-aboard boat from Semporna or take a 45-minute speedboat journey to the resorts on Pulau Kapalai or Pulau Mabul.

WATER TEMPERATURE
Average 27°C (81°F).

QUALITY OF MARINE LIFE
Very good with a high density of stony and soft corals, gorgonias, other invertebrates and both reef and pelagic fish including sharks.

DEPTH OF DIVES
From the surface to depths well beyond the accepted limits of sport diving – act responsibly.

SAFETY
Currents are mostly mild but can be strong.

MUCK DIVING
BORNEO

The success of Pulau Sipadan and the limits put on the accommodation due to its marine park status led to the establishment of diving resorts on many nearby islands and reefs, particularly Pulau Kapalai and Pulau Mabul, which are only 15-minutes away.

Both Pulau Kapalai and Pulau Mabul are 45-minutes by speedboat south of Semporna on the northeast coast of Sabah and Pulau Sipadan is 15-minutes further on.

First coined by Bob Halstead in Papua New Guinea, 'Muck Diving' is diving over a silty, sandy or coral rubble seabed. Concentrated observation locates tiny colourful creatures camouflaged against their environment. Having realized the possibilities, divers soon found creatures that they thought had been missing in Indonesia's Lembeh Strait, Borneo's Pulau Kapalai, Pulau Mabul and Pulau Lankayan and in the Philippines' Anilao, Boracay, Puerto Galera and Malapascua. Quite often, no one had bothered to look for such small creatures before so it is likely that they are found on most reefs if divers look hard enough.

PULAU KAPALAI

Pulau Kapalai is like living over an aquarium, it is only 15-minutes from Pulau Sipadan but the diving is completely different. Flamboyant cuttlefish flash brilliant black, maroon, yellow and red colours that make them stand out against the sand. Nearby, but so well camouflaged that they are much more difficult to find, harlequin ghost pipefish hide among the branches of similarly coloured Gorgonian sea fans, a seagrass ghost pipefish hides among the weeds and a tiny bright-red frogfish hides

against a sponge. Every evening mating mandarinfish cavort under the jetty at dusk.

Searching Gorgonian whip corals with a small dive light, divers find tiny, almost-transparent, commensal gobies and shrimps camouflaged among the feeding polyps. Anemones, bubble corals, Dendronephthya soft tree corals, sea cucumbers and cushion stars harbour tiny shrimps and crabs living in symbiosis while sea horses hide among algae. Add blue-ringed and mimic octopuses, flying gurnards, crab-eye gobies, sea moths, jawfish, snake eels and many colourful nudibranchs and you get an idea of the joys of muck diving.

Well-camouflaged among the coral are weedy

Right A diver using flash to photograph mixed stony corals at Ikon's Rock, Pulau Lankayan

UNDERWATER VISIBILITY

In mid-oceanic waters the vertical visibility can reach 100 m (328ft), but horizontal visibility greater than 50-60 m (165-197 ft) is mythical. Coastal waters are affected by rain, run-off, disturbed bottom sediment, agricultural, industrial and domestic pollution, landfill, quarrying, volcanic eruptions and plankton blooms so the visibility is lower. Water clarity is better over deep water or a solid bottom. Ebb tides lower water clarity by carrying sediment off beaches and reefs, visibility usually improves on a flood tide. Care with buoyancy will stop divers from disturbing the bottom sediment.

Heavy rain and wind lowers the visibility if bad weather causes the freshwater and salt water to mix, or it sets off a plankton bloom.

Offshore waters appear blue but the decaying organic matter in coastal waters is yellow so some of the blue light is filtered-out and the waters look green. Local mineral deposits or mining can also affect the colour of the water.

PACIFIC OCEAN

scorpionfish (*Rhinopias frondosa*). The Holy Grail of many underwater photographers, this 'King of Critters', a favourite with divers looking for the rare, weird and unusual, is just another of the myriad of fascinating subjects found on these reefs.

PULAU LANKAYAN

Much further north at 6° 30' N / 117° 55' E, a two hour speedboat journey north-northwest of Sandakan near to the border with the Philippines in the Sulu Sea, the latest diving destination to be developed off the east coast of Sabah is Pulau Lankayan. An even smaller island than Pulau Sipadan, Pulau Lankayan is covered with lush vegetation. This muck diving paradise lies among several large but shallow reefs replete with reef and pelagic species. Whale sharks pass by in late March and early April and the occasional dugong has been seen.

The reefs are a mixture of sandy areas on gentle slopes down to 25 m (82 ft) with large barrel sponges, Gorgonian sea fans and whip corals, fields of lettuce corals, staghorn Acropora corals and large Porites coral heads. There can be strong surface currents. Visibility varies with the reef dived and the state of the tide; 25 m (82 ft) is considered good. The smaller creatures here are much the same as those at Pulau Kapalai with the addition of species specific to the Sulu Sea including a larger species of jawfish, at Jawfish Lair. Large and small nudibranchs are everywhere, batfish, barracuda, sweetlips and large groupers follow divers around.

Below A 3cm (1 in)-long spotted frogfish camouflaged alongside a red sponge, Pulau Kapalai

Massive spiny lobsters peek out from under overhangs, devil scorpionfish, leaf scorpionfish, ribbon eels, mantis shrimps and true giant clams are common.

Green and hawksbill turtles use the beaches for nesting. Local wrecks include the purposely sunk Lankayan Wreck, an ocean-going fishing vessel that was caught poaching and what is left of an armed barge of the Japanese Mosquito Fleet, sunk during World War II. Made of wood, the fishing boat is now breaking up but it can be entered with care and has profuse fish and invertebrate life including groupers, emperor snappers, longhorn boxfish, sweetlips and large *Discodoris boholensis* nudibranchs.

Without the local divemasters and their intimate knowledge of the terrain and each animal's behaviour, most divers would miss many of the small creatures. Every hole contains something interesting but many exciting subjects are not actually in holes, they just depended on excellent camouflage. To experienced divers who can accept that visibility does not always have to be exceptional, these destinations are as good as it gets.

FACTS

CLIMATE
Climate: 26–30ºC (80–86ºF), tropical, warm and humid all year and rarely below 20ºC (68ºF).

SEASONALITY
The islands can be dived year-round but the weather is best from May–October. August is the high season for both local holidays and turtle nesting.

GETTING THERE
To visit the islands around Pulau Sipadan fly to Kota Kinabalu, then take a domestic flight to Tawau. Then go by road to Semporna. Divers can visit Pulau Sipadan by boat or live-aboard boat from Semporna or take a 45-minute speedboat journey to the resorts on Pulau Kapalai or Pulau Mabul.

To visit Pulau Lankayan fly to Kota Kinabalu, then take a domestic flight to Sandakan. Pulau Lankayan is a two hour speedboat journey north-northwest of Sandakan.

WATER TEMPERATURE
Average 27°C (81°F).

QUALITY OF MARINE LIFE
Very good, a high density of stony and soft corals, gorgonias, other invertebrates and both reef and pelagic fish including Sharks.

DEPTH OF DIVES
Dives are within 5-30 m (16-98 ft).

SAFETY
Currents are mostly mild but can be strong.

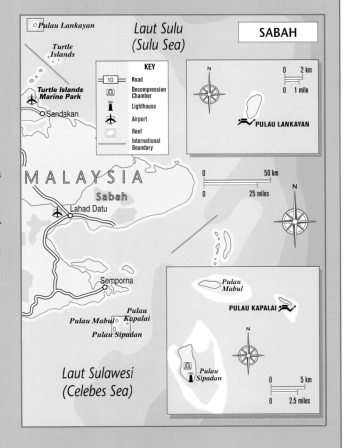

STRONG CURRENTS

THE PHILIPPINES

The Philippines is an archipelago of 7,107 islands and islets, of which only 2,000 are inhabited. The irregular, rugged coastline extends 35,000 km (21,700 miles), with numerous natural harbours, sandy beaches and 34,000 sq km (13,127 sq miles) of coral reefs.

In many places the tides sweep across vast areas of the Pacific Ocean with no land in the way to slow them down before they eddy around the islands. With a 2.2 m (7 ft) tidal range in six hours at Puerto Galera, the better diving operators understand tide tables and use these stronger currents to good effect.

Easy to reach from Manila, Puerto Galera on the north of Mindoro Island is the Philippines' busiest diving destination. Situated on a beautiful natural harbour, with many fine beaches and sheltered coves, Puerto Galera, which translates as the Port of Galleons, has been a port since the 10th century, where ships could shelter safely from typhoons.

The diving off Puerto Galera is famous for its diversity. There are all standards, from easy dives for training and novices, to high-voltage drift-dives in strong currents and some deep dives where larger animals are encountered. Thresher sharks have been seen between 20 and 40 m (66 and 131 ft) from December to March; their appearance usually coincides with the arrival of shoals of tuna and mackerel. Threshers can be large but are not considered dangerous to divers and tend to be very shy.

In recent years several wrecks have been sunk for divers and technical diving has become common. Puerto Galera was already known for its macro photography but some operators have been looking harder and finding most of the critters that muck divers enthuse about including frogfish, pygmy seahorses, stargazers, ribbon eels, leaf scorpionfish, ghost pipefish, porcelain crabs, anemone shrimps, nudibranchs, mantis shrimps, fire gobies, harlequin shrimps and flamboyant cuttlefish.

THE CANYONS

The most popular dive in Puerto Galera is The Canyons; an advanced dive due to the depth and strong currents, this is the place in Puerto Galera for big fish action.

At The Canyons, divers require a knowledgeable local dive guide to show them where to correctly enter the water to allow the current to carry them to the right places as once in the current they are committed. Starting on a flood tide just west of Puerto Galera's Escarceo Point, they drop into 9 m (30 ft) of water, with fields of acropora table corals and race over several stepped drop-offs to reach the Hole In The Wall. This small hole, covered in multicoloured *Dendronephthya* soft tree corals, sponges and crinoids and home to frogfish, scorpionfish, lionfish and trumpetfish, leads to The Canyons. Swept on by the current past an area teeming with fish, they rush around Escarceo Point into a bowl shaped depression at 40 m (131 ft) known as The Fish Bowl where they look down at an abundance of shoaling fish and their predators. Whitetip reef sharks, grey reef sharks, large tuna, shoals of rainbow runners, batfish, snappers, oriental sweetlips, spotted sweetlips, fusiliers, trevallies, batfish, bluespotted ribbontail rays and barracuda as well as lone groupers. Triggerfish, surgeonfish, filefish and giant trevallies mill around. Every hole in the stony coral seems to contain a redtooth

Right Large stony corals provide perfect hiding places for small reef fish

THE REEF AT WAR

The coral make up of a reef is constantly changing. Storms, freshwater floods, siltation and changes in currents, sea levels or water temperature, as well as disease, predation and the excesses of man, can kill corals. Faster growing corals may block out the sunlight falling on other corals and table corals eventually snap under their own weight.

Corals exposed to air during low water secrete a heavy mucous coating, which helps to prevent dehydration. This is the oily slick that is seen floating away on a rising tide.

Many species compete for the best areas down to 30 m (98 ft), so they have devised methods to defend their territory or to expand at the expense of other species.

In areas of strong current, corals that have many branching arms are prevalent; their shape slows down the water flow over their polyps, giving them more chance to catch prey. Acropora corals, have more species, grow faster and occupy more reef area than any other species.

When some corals detect a competing coral nearby, they grow extra long tentacles in that direction, with a higher concentration of nematocysts. These tentacles wave about in the direction of the intruder and kill it on touch.

Over distances of less than 2 cm (0.8 inches), some corals open a hole in their body wall and send out digestive filaments to digest intruders.

Coral reefs give home and shelter to many marine creatures, but are themselves preyed upon. Planktonic shrimps, crabs and mussels feed on their mucus and certain starfish, urchins, crabs and fish eat the coral tissue.

Predators preying on coral tissue, such as butterflyfish, cause the other tentacles to retract, so they do not seriously damage any one colony before being forced to move on to another. Some triggerfish eat both tissue and skeleton, but not in large quantities. More serious is the damage done by crown-of-thorns starfish and bumphead parrotfish.

Crown-of-thorns starfish kill large areas of coral, especially when their populations explode. They often return to the same specimen every night until the whole colony is dead. They mainly prey on fast growing acropora corals. Bumphead parrotfish occur in large shoals with some individuals exceeding 1 m (3.3 ft) in length; they charge into the coral, breaking it off with their forehead, consuming both tissue and skeleton.

Soft corals and gorgonian corals usually lose out when competing with reef building corals in well-lit water except where their flexibility makes them self cleaning in areas of high siltation. They manage better in poorly lit locations, in caves, under overhangs or in deep water.

Gorgonian sea fans do best in strong currents where their position at right angles to the current, and construction, with polyps so close as to be almost touching, slows down the current enough for their tentacles to trap prey.

Human sewage adds to siltation and often spreads disease, industry discharges toxic chemicals, shipwrecks can leak oil for decades, crude oil is toxic and its heavier constituents eventually sink, smothering corals and bottom-dwelling creatures. Detergents and agricultural fertilizers release nitrates and phosphates, which contribute to algal blooms that poison fish and people, smother corals and cut out sunlight.

Anchors, divers and swimmers kill corals that they touch or break, fortunately many marine parks supply fixed moorings and environmentally aware captains set up their own, though often only to have them stolen by local fishermen.

Despite the doom and gloom of some ill-informed magazines, coral reefs are surviving but they do need our help – we must clean up our act to enable them to survive.

Left A crown-of-thorns sea star preying on coral, French Polynesia, Pacific

triggerfish, there are shoals of anthias and crinoids of many colours are out sifting the current for food.

Manta rays, lone thresher sharks and scalloped hammerhead sharks have been seen in the winter so divers should look up and out to sea as well as down.

Dragged along by the current, the divers fight their way into the shelter of some large rocks, check out several moray eels and octopuses and then move around the corner where the current picks up again and sweeps them on into The Canyons. The Canyons can be used to shelter from the current, the first canyon is to 26 m (85 ft), the second canyon is to 28 m (92 ft) and has great Gorgonian sea fans while the third is deeper and often has a shoal of snappers using it for shelter. After the third canyon the coral and fish life becomes prolific again but is exposed to the current; the same varied species as at The Fish Bowl with the addition of six-banded angelfish, regal angelfish and emperor angelfish and butterflyfish. The deeper water has large barrel sponges, Gorgonian sea whips, Gorgonian sea fans and occasionally turtles.

If they manage to get the current right, the divers are eventually swept onto an old, coral encrusted 1.5 m (5 ft) anchor at 26 m (85 ft), it may have come from a wreck or simply have been abandoned. The divers can hang on to this anchor while the group gathers together again. When they let go they are swept away in the current and ascend slowly to decompress in open water.

As high-voltage drift-dives go, The Canyons is one of the best, but be warned, the currents can be fierce at the peak of a flood tide and difficult on an ebb tide. photographers should aim to dive as near as possible to slack water.

The only problem with The Canyons dive site is its depth – bottom time is short. This is a world-class dive that divers will want to repeat again and again.

Left Juvenile pinnate spadefish (batfish) at Pulau Sipadan

FACTS

CLIMATE
23–36°C (73–97°F), tropical, with pronounced seasons: dry November–February, wet June–October, when typhoons can occur.

SEASONALITY
All year round with the peak season being December–June.

GETTING THERE
Puerto Galera is easily reached from Manila in 4-5 hours by travelling by road to Batangas and then taking a ferry.

WATER TEMPERATURE
25–31°C (77–88°F).

QUALITY OF MARINE LIFE
There is great biodiversity, a high density of stony and soft corals, gorgonias, other invertebrates and both reef and pelagic fish including sharks.

DEPTH OF DIVES
40 m (131 ft), but divers can go to depths well beyond the accepted limits of sport diving here, so act responsibly.

SAFETY
Currents are strong and can be fierce.

WRECK DIVING
THE PHILIPPINES

Rich in wrecks, waters around the Philippines include the remains of galleons that carried rich cargoes and junks that carried valuable ceramics. Most of these have been salvaged either commercially or pirated by local people.

However, recreational divers are more interested in more modern vessels, most of which were sunk in World War II. These vessels include those found at Subic Bay, several Japanese ships found around Busuanga and Coron Islands in the Calamian Group and two at Pearl Farm, Davao, on Mindanao Island.

Subic Bay is best known for the old Armoured Cruiser ex-USS *New York*, which was commissioned on August 1st, 1893. In a long illustrious career she was renamed as the USS *Saratoga* and later renamed again as the USS *Rochester*.

However, as a condensed version of Chuuk (Truk) Lagoon, it is the area around Busuanga Island and Coron Island at the northern tip of Palawan that attracts wreck fanatics from around the world.

In 1944, Admiral 'Bull' Halsey ordered reconnaissance aircraft to photograph the Linapacan Strait to check out the Japanese firepower in preparation for the American landing on Leyte and the Calamian islands. When an observant mapping officer noticed that some of the islands moved about, they realized that they had found a camouflaged Japanese fleet. At 09:00 hours on September 24th, carrier-based Grumman Hellcat and Helldiver aircraft of Task Force 38 attacked and sank at least 18 vessels around Busuanga Island.

Today, 14 of these wrecks have been located and together with some more recent civilian vessels and a wooden fishing boat, have become havens for divers, including: The *Nanshin Maru* (Black Island Wreck), which sits upright down a sandy slope on the east-side of Malajon (Black) Island. A vessel that is either the *Okikawa Maru* or the *Taiei Maru*, south of Concepción village on Busuanga Island. The flying boat tender IJN *Akitsushima*, which lies between Lajo Island and Manglet Island. A salvaged, shallow gunboat, which lies at the southern end of Lusong Island. An unknown freighter, which lies between the northern end of Lusong Island and Tangat Island. The freighter *Kogyo Maru*, which lies on her starboard side south of the unknown freighter, east of the southeast corner of Lusong Island.

The refrigerated provision ship *Irako*, which lies on its starboard side southeast of Lusong Island. The freighter *Olympia Maru*, which lies on its starboard side west of the southwest end of Tangat Island. The East Tangat Wreck, which lists to starboard down a sandy slope southeast of the east side of Tangat Island.

And further north, the freighter *Kyokuzan Maru*, which is also known as the Dimilanta Wreck, sits almost upright northeast of Busuanga Island.

Although a lot of these vessels' cargo and some engines have been salvaged, the whole area is a miniature Truk Lagoon.

THE IJN *AKITSUSHIMA*

Between Lajo Island and Manglet Island, south of Concepción village on Busuanga Island, the IJN *Akitsushima* is the only true warship in this area as the others were mostly auxiliary vessels.

The Imperial Japanese Navy (IJN) *Akitsushima* Flying-boat Tender was ordered for the Japanese Navy in the 1939 Programme, laid down in 1940 and launched on

Right Lionfish against the *Nanshin Maru* wreck, Malajon Island, Coron Bay

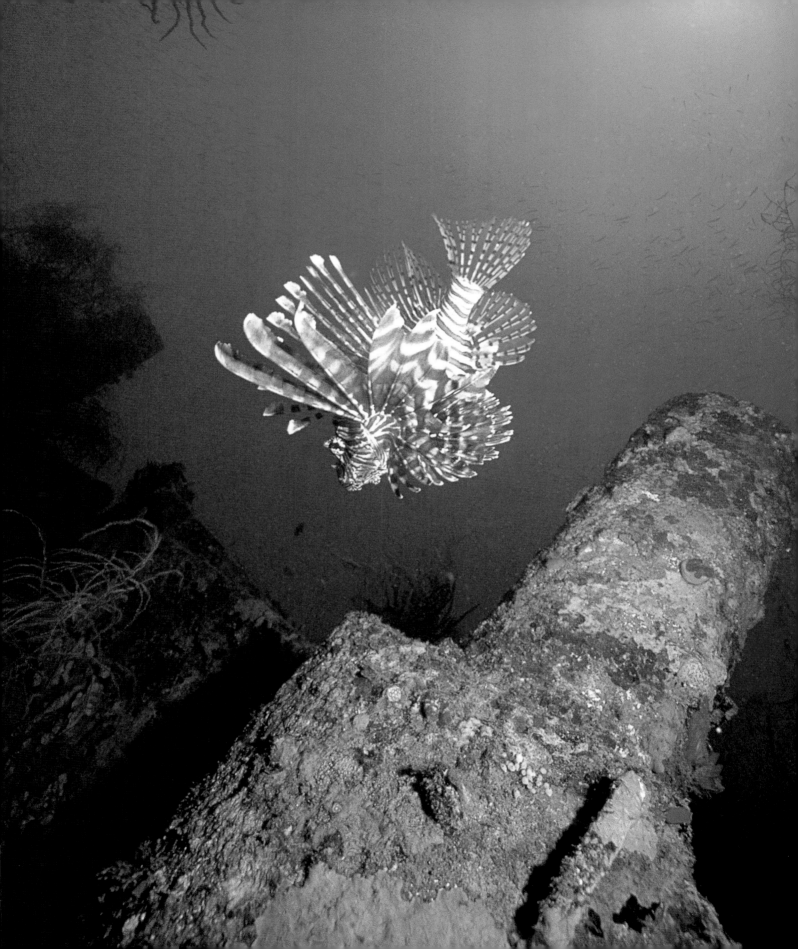

GUNTER'S CATHEDRAL

A unique dive into a hidden, beautiful cavern. The entrance to Gunter's cathedral is in the water north-north east of Calis Point on Coron Island, where several undercut limestone cliffs lead to small caves and keyholes. Having found the large cavern entrance, the secret is finding a narrow cleft in the floor that leads to the Cathedral cavern.

Divers begin by swimming over fallen, coral-encrusted rocks to the large, outer cavern. This cavern is not obvious so they will need an experienced divemaster to point out where it is. The bottom of this main cavern entrance is at 7–8 m (23–26 ft). They then locate and descend an apparently dead end narrow cleft in the floor of this cavern and find a tube-like, man-sized tunnel at the bottom. This tunnel is dark and quite narrow and goes through two bends, it is very easy for it to silt up and have zero visibility if the divers are clumsy or a swell gets up.

The divers continue through this tunnel admiring spiny lobsters and cowrie shells overhead and continue, at first in complete darkness but later towards a gleam of light ahead. They eventually exit the tunnel at the bottom of a chamber some 20 m (66 ft) high and slightly narrower in width – Gunter's Cathedral.

Gunter's Cathedral is beautiful, particularly when shafts of sunlight descend almost vertically through the water from a large hole in the roof. A large tree had been growing here until it broke the roof away and fell into the chamber. The chamber itself is about one third full of water, rubble and silt, so you can rise to the surface and chat to each other in air.

If novices wish to try this dive they should have steady nerves, not suffer claustrophobia and be accompanied by an

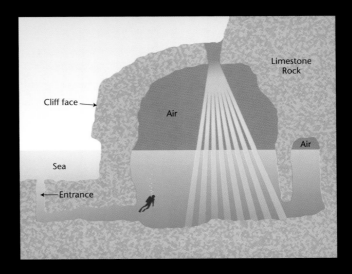

experienced local divemaster. Finding the way out again can become extremely difficult if the large mound of sediment at the bottom of the chamber is stirred up by the divers, the swell or changes in the tide. With less experienced divers, the divemaster should treat the dive as a cave dive and position a safety line through the tunnel first, the other divers can then feel their way in and out along this safety line.

There is interesting though not spectacular coral, outside under the boat and some true giant clams (*Tridacna gigas*), for those wary of going into the Cathedral.

Left Sunlight penetrates Gunter's Cathedral via a gap in the ceiling

133

April 25th, 1941 at the Kawasaki Shipyard at Kobe, Japan. The vessel was completed on April 29th, 1942. She was built for the specific purpose of operating one large flying boat. This *Akitsushima* should not be confused with the armoured cruiser of the same name that was built by the Yokosuka Naval Arsenal and scrapped on January 10th, 1927.

Previously lucky in surviving other US hits in air attacks including 'Operation Hailstorm' in Chuuk (Truk) Lagoon, the *Akitsushima* was sunk in the air raid on Coron by Task Force 38, the flying boat *Kawanishi* H8K1 'Emily' was never found.

The *Akitsushima*, 4,650 gross tons, 118 m (387 ft)-long, 15.8 m (52 ft)-beam and 5.4 m (18 ft)-draft, now lies on its port side pointing 290 degrees (compass bearing) in 38 m (125 ft) of water, with the starboard side hull at 20 m (66 ft).

The arm of the stern crane that was used to load and unload the flying boat lies broken, to port, in 34 m (112 ft) of water. The main deck is split near the stern between this crane and the funnel, with the ship almost torn into two leaving considerable internal damage.

An advanced dive due to the depth, the vessel can be penetrated with care by qualified wreck divers or those accompanied by an instructor, but be careful of sharp metal resulting from the explosions. Experienced wreck divers can almost swim from bow to stern inside the wreck along many corridors. They can penetrate into the engine room to view the two shaft-geared diesel engines that gave the vessel a speed of 19 knots. The machinery for operating the crane can be found at the stern. A three-barreled anti-aircraft gun mounting is at the front of the flying boat tracks.

When strong currents occur the IJN *Akitsushima* is not a dive for the inexperienced.

Left The wooden fishing boat wreck near Barracuda Lake, Coron Island

FACTS

CLIMATE
Tropical, temperature 23-36°C (73-97°F).

SEASONALITY
All year round but best dived from December to June.

GETTING THERE
Fly by light aircraft or take ferry from Manila to Busuanga Island, then by road to the resort or live-aboard boat.

WATER TEMPERATURE
25-31°C (77-88°F).

QUALITY OF MARINE LIFE
Very good, a high density of stony and soft corals, gorgonias, other invertebrates and both reef and pelagic fish.

DEPTH OF DIVES
38 m (125 ft).

SAFETY
Currents can be strong.

BIG FISH
THE PHILIPPINES

The Sulu Sea has hundreds of isolated reefs and islets with diving as good as anywhere in the world. Unfortunately some of them are so remote that they can only be visited for four months of the year because of the weather.

The name *Tubbataha* is the Samal peoples' word for "long reef exposed at low tide". The Cagayanen people who are more geographically associated with the Tubbataha Reefs refer to Tubbataha as *gusong*. Although the sea is usually calm with some swell, there are normally strong currents that can take divers in either direction and often change quite suddenly. If you do not mind currents, then here is where you will find the Philippines' best diving, with large animals guaranteed. This is strictly a live-aboard destination and it can have very bad weather. A strong gale onboard a boat can be a terrifying experience so you should choose a heavy, broad-beamed vessel.

You must expect strong currents. If the current is not strong it will probably pick up or reverse during the course of your dive, or as you round a corner. The live-aboard's chase boats will follow your bubbles, but it is worth carrying a bright orange or yellow delayed deployment surface marker buoy or rescue tube and an old CD to use as a heliograph.

All dives are exciting drift-dives with many large species and large shoals to observe. Divers are not swept through any dangerous terrain, just along the wall or over the edge of the reef. The best time for diving is March through June, but bad weather can occur at any time. Novices should stay close to their divemaster and good chase boat cover is essential.

182 km (98 nautical miles) southeast of Puerto Princesa on Palawan Island, the Tubbataha and Jessie Beazley Reefs are at the centre of the Sulu-Sulawesi Marine Ecoregion (SSME), and at the apex of the Coral Triangle, the world's epicentre of marine life. 23 km (12 nautical miles) northwest of Tubbataha North Islet, Jessie Beazley Reef is a mound of broken coral surrounded by white sand and reef.

All of these reefs consist of vertical walls or near vertical drop-offs, rising out of the depths. Jessie

Right A large shoal of trevallies off Tubbataha Reef

TUBBATAHA REEF NATIONAL MARINE PARK

Tubbataha Reef National Marine Park forms part of the Palawan Biosphere Reserve and was inscribed on the UNESCO World Heritage List in 1993.

The Tubbataha reefs consist of two extensive, atoll-like reefs, with inner lagoons, separated by a 7 km (4 nautical mile) channel. At low water there are several sand cays. At the northeast end of the north reef is Bird Islet, a cay with sand, grass and some mangroves, used as a rookery by Brown Boobies and terns and as a nesting beach by turtles. The South Islet has a prominent black rock and some sandy cays at the northeast end and a solar powered lighthouse at the southern end. Gulls and terns nest by the lighthouse. To the east of the lighthouse, high and dry on the reef, lies the disintegrating wreck of the *Delsan*, an old log carrier.

Originally covering 33,220 ha (82 acres), on August 23, 2006, Jessie Beazley Reef and waters in between were included within the expanded Tubbataha Reefs Natural Park (TRNP). Now the park covers 96,828 ha (239 acres), almost three times its initial size.

Beazley Reef North and South have most of the large shoals of fish while the Tubbataha reefs have more of the larger fish.

On Jessie Beazley Reef, the reef as a whole but especially the Southern End, has diving that is as good as it gets. The currents here can take you either way along the drop-off and the reef is small enough to be covered in two dives with these currents.

On Tubbataha Reef's North Islet – the North Face, East Face, Southwest Corner (Amos Rock), and Southeast Corner, and on Tubbataha Reef's South Islet – the North/Northeast End and South/Southwest End, are all among the best dives in the world for fish species.

TUBBATAHA REEF – NORTH ISLET – EAST FACE

The top of this reef is a rich slope of corals on sand dropping to between 14 m (46 ft) and 20 m (66 ft), the reef then drops as a wall or drop-off with overhangs, caves and crevices down to depths deeper than sports divers should dive on air. The reef top is particularly good

Below A large, resting tawny nurse shark in a cave, Tubbataha North Reef, Sulu Sea

for lettuce, staghorn and table corals, leathery corals, whip corals and sponges that are teeming with parrotfish, rabbitfish, hawkfish, anthias, boxfish and fire gobies among everything else. Every hole seems to be home to a redtooth triggerfish. In many places, bluespotted ribbontail rays, spiny lobsters and turtles are seen near to the surface while resting zebra (leopard) sharks and guitar sharks are common on the sand. Pelagic visitors are possible at any time.

The walls are covered in huge barrel sponges, colourful gorgonias including gorgonian sea fans, soft corals, hydroids, black corals and Tubastrea corals. Some horizontal caves in the walls contain resting nurse sharks or groups of whitetip reef sharks, but it is off the walls in deeper water that this reef shows its true worth. Shoals of angelfish, butterflyfish, rainbow runners, moorish idols, fusiliers, trevallies, snappers and sweetlips follow you around. Large trevally, tuna and barracuda come out of the blue, grey reef sharks and whitetip reef sharks patrol, giant manta rays fly overhead, and eagle rays and turtles pass by. Massive groupers, humphead (Napoleon) wrasse, large pufferfish and squirrelfish hover around.

There are large numbers of longjawed (sabre) squirrelfish, Zaizer's bigeyes, midnight snappers, black snappers, Vlaming's unicornfish, rainbow runners, emperors, pennant bannerfish, batfish, spotted and lined sweetlips, angelfish, especially royal, emperor and yellowmask or blue-face. The triggerfish include clown triggerfish and there are often grey and whitetip reef sharks resting on the sand at the base of the wall.

There are many species of nudibranchs, flat worms, segmented worms, sea cucumbers, sea stars, sea squirts, feather duster worms, sea urchins, sea cucumbers, garden eels and of course, colourful crinoids everywhere. The wall's gorgonian sea fans and soft corals are very large below 30 m (98 ft).

If divers avoid the times of very strong currents, (spring tides), this site is a good dusk dive, when there is plenty of noisy action as predatory fish are on the prowl. Night dives are very good if the current is weak. Visibility can reach 40 m (131 ft), the average depth is 20 m (65 ft) and the maximum depth is beyond 60 m (197 ft).

FACTS

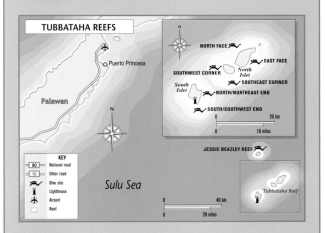

CLIMATE
Tropical with temperatures of 23–36ºC (73–97ºF).

SEASONALITY
March through June.

GETTING THERE
Fly to Puerto Princesa on Palawan, then continue on a live-aboard boat.

WATER TEMPERATURE
25–31ºC (77–88ºF).

QUALITY OF MARINE LIFE
Diverse and prolific, a high density of stony and soft corals, gorgonias, other invertebrates and both reef and large pelagic fish including Sharks.

DEPTH OF DIVES
From the surface to depths well beyond the accepted limits of recreational sport diving but there is no need to go beyond 40 m (131 ft).

SAFETY
Currents are strong and can be fierce.

BIG FISH, THE PHILIPPINES

WHALE SHARKS
THAILAND

To dive with the largest fish in the sea is as exciting as diving or snorkelling gets. They are often quite easy to approach but usually move on too quickly for divers to follow and keep up.

Accompanied by large remoras, cobia and juvenile trevallies, these majestic animals, the size of a small bus, can move remarkably quickly. However, if divers behave quietly in the water, the whale sharks will approach them as if they are as interested in the divers as the divers are in them. This is particularly so of juveniles.

Whale sharks are seen in all of Thailand's Andaman Sea, they appear to migrate northwards from the Malaysian border during January and February to reach the border with Myanmar (Burma) during February, March and April. Areas where whale shark sightings are common include near to the northern end of the Strait of Malacca at Hin Mouang and nearby Hin Daeng 37 km (23 miles) south-southwest of Koh Lanta Yai and to the north, 14 km (9 miles) east-southeast of the Surin Island's Koh Surin Tai at Richelieu Rock. All three sites are relatively small reef structures in a large expanse of open sea where currents striking the pinnacles produce upwellings that bring nutrient-rich water containing plankton up from the seabed. As well as being food for many reef fish, this plankton attracts whale sharks and manta rays that often stay around for extended periods.

These pinnacles are remarkable in often having everything from macro critters to the largest fish in the sea so on all of these dive sites, divers checking out the marine life on the wall should make sure that they also keep an eye on the open water for big fish.

The name of Hin Mouang (Purple Rock) comes from the purple anemones and Dendronephthya soft tree corals on top of the most prominent pinnacle and that of Hin Daeng (Red Rock) comes from the colourful Dendronephthya soft tree corals.

One of the best dive sites in Thailand, Hin Mouang is completely submerged and is very rich in marine life along a collection of submerged pinnacles nearly 200 m (656 ft)-long but barely 20 m (66 ft)-wide. The main structure heads southwest with the shallowest pinnacles rising to 8 m (26 ft) from the surface. The deep drop-off exceeds 70 m (230 ft). The fish life includes a variety of large pelagic creatures, whale sharks, silvertip sharks, barracuda, tuna, large stingrays and what for Thai waters are large groups of grey reef sharks.

Nearby Hin Daeng is easier to find as it breaks the surface at low tide. Although not quite as rich in marine life as its neighbour it is still very good with a series of walls and shelves. Hin Daeng is another magnet for whale sharks, manta rays and other pelagic species as well as reef fish including large groups of timid grey reef sharks and a few zebra (leopard) sharks and nurse sharks.

Divers have noticed over the years that the whale sharks and manta rays tend to favour one or the other of these two sites at any one given time, so it is always best to check out both sites.

Probably the best known dive site in Thailand, Richelieu Rock is a rock pinnacle rising steeply from 33 m (108 ft) to break the surface at low tide 14 km (9 miles) east-southeast of the Surin Island's Koh Surin Tai. The name translates from the French as 'rich place', and may have come from fishermen travelling from what used to be called French Indo-China.

Right A diver swimming next to a whale shark at Richelieu Rock

Richelieu Rock is shaped like a shortened horseshoe with a main central outcrop surrounded by smaller, submerged pinnacles the tops of which range from as shallow as 3 m (10ft) down to 10 m (33ft). The pinnacles themselves have numerous shelves and ledges at all depths and the main outcrop is small enough to be circled four or five times in a single dive.

The currents at Richelieu Rock can be strong but the leeside of the pinnacle can be used for shelter so there is always a protected side. Even when there are no whale sharks present there is still plenty to see, by circling the rock in an upward spiral, divers can view an amazing diversity of marine life from blue spotted ribbontail rays, requiem, zebra (leopard) and guitar Sharks to huge shoals

Below Diver swimming with a whale shark off Richelieu Rock

of barracuda, trevallies, rainbow runners, reef fish including huge groupers, surgeonfish, scorpionfish, frogfish, cuttlefish, octopuses, sea horses, moray eels, anemones with various species of clownfish, barrel sponges, Dendronephthya soft tree corals and gorgonian sea fans. In addition every nook and cranny houses a macro critter including nudibranchs, lobsters and shrimps.

Sometimes, while the divers are resting between dives, a whale shark will swim around the dive boat for 10-15 minutes, usually long enough for the divers to don fins, mask and snorkel and get a close look at the animal.

Richelieu Rock has the greatest frequency of whale shark sightings in Thai waters, and on occasion occurs as two or three animals are seen at the same time.

Other areas of the world such as Western Australia and the Seychelles are famous for whale sharks but nowadays visitors hoping to encounter these animals are limited to snorkelling with them. The major difference in diving at these three sites in Thailand is that divers do not require spotter planes to find them – the sharks are attracted to and cruise around the pinnacles.

FACTS

CLIMATE
Dominated by the NE and SW monsoons. The NE monsoon gives reasonable weather in the Andaman Sea from December to May but the SW monsoon, May to October, can give rough weather at sea. Temperatures 21-34°C (70-93°F).

SEASONALITY
Best dived from December to May.

GETTING THERE
There are international flights to Phuket from where you take a live-aboard boat.

WATER TEMPERATURE
27-31°C (75-88°F).

QUALITY OF MARINE LIFE
Very good, a high density of stony and soft corals, gorgonias, other invertebrates and both reef and pelagic fish including sharks.

DEPTH OF DIVES
From 5 m (16 ft) to depths well beyond the accepted limits of sport diving, so act responsibly.

SAFETY
Currents are strong and can be fierce.

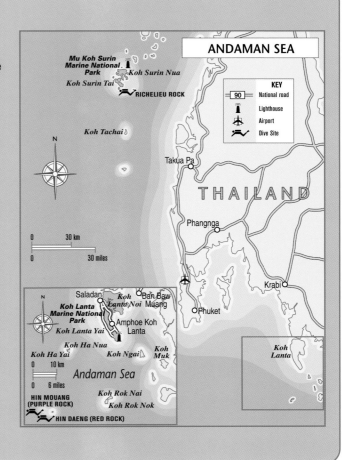

MUCK DIVING
INDONESIA

Spread across the equator, the Indian and Pacific Oceans and the Wallace line, the hypothetical boundary between Australian and Southeast Asian fauna, Indonesia is the world's largest archipelago.

No one really knows how many islands Indonesia has and it varies with the state of the tide, but the figure often quoted is 17,508 islands with about 6,000 of these being inhabited. It consists of five major islands and about 30 smaller groups spreading 5,150 km (3,200 miles) from Sumatra in the west to West Papua (formerly Irian Jaya) in the east, with almost 80,000 km (49,712 miles) of coastline.

The Lembeh Strait is a narrow channel, about 14 km (9 miles)-long and 1-2 km (0.6-1.2 miles)-wide. While the general diversity of the area is caused by the unique geographic position of the strait, its particular diversity at any one place is influenced by the different underwater habitats present. Although black volcanic sand slopes are the norm, there are white limestone sandy slopes, shipwrecks, patches of rubble and reefs with colourful soft corals. The northern and southern entrances to the strait have coral reefs, and there are shallows along the sides. Each particular habitat supports a different set of marine organisms and it is not unusual to see a number of different sea horses, pygmy sea horses, frogfish, leaf scorpionfish, mimic octopus, wonderpus octopus, ghost pipefish, flamboyant cuttlefish and countless nudibranchs in just one dive.

There are over 30 dive sites around the straits, mostly either sandy areas or small reefs but also shipwrecks. Most of the diving is searching for well-camouflaged,

rare, and weird species, so divers will be dependent on a local dive guide to point out the likely subjects.

HAIRBALL

Two similar sites that offer true muck diving with lots of critters on black sand slopes with algae and the occasional patch of sponges. Some of the animals found here grow skin filaments to blend in with the algae and the site is so named because of the impression of the weed lying on the black volcanic sand. Common

Right A spiny sea urchin illuminated in a diver's light

THE USE OF BLAST FISHING

Blast fishing has occurred in most parts of the world: it was once common in the Mediterranean, is still common in some African lakes and rivers, poachers have used it on salmon, soldiers have used hand grenades in the Red Sea and emigrants took it with them to Australia and North America. It is now rare in Europe, but despite its illegality, it is still common in remote Pacific islands, Indonesia, the Philippines, and areas of Malaysia close to Indonesia and the Philippines.

Blast fishing is extremely wasteful, as not all the dead fish float so it is usually performed in shallow water. Young fish are killed before they reach reproductive age as are other non-edible creatures.

The worst damage is to the coral, which is the environment and the protective habitat that gives shelter to many small marine creatures which are essential to the health of the ecosystem and food for larger inhabitants. Coral damage by blast fishing also contributes to ciguatera poisoning. Sadly for the poor peasant fisherman, feeding his family today is more important than saving the environment for tomorrow, but on the brighter side the advent of higher earnings from tourism may yet save many reefs.

Above The mantis shrimp, a classic 'critter', Lembeh Straits

sights are frogfish, Ambon scorpionfish, snake eels, devilfish, sea horses, octopuses and flamboyant cuttlefish. The deepest point is 30 m (98 ft) and the shallowest has sea urchins at 3 m (10 ft). There is lots of discarded rubbish from the nearby village but all of the interest is in or on the sand.

BATU KAPAL

This dive site is different from most other dive sites at Lembeh Strait because it is at the north end of Lembeh Island and therefore is not in the narrows of the strait. Divers who are not addicted to muck diving would consider it the best dive site here.

Batu Kapal is set of pinnacles lying off the northern end of Lembeh Island and divers begin at 24 m (79 ft) at the base of the pinnacle of Batu Kapal itself and then follow a ridge northeast to a large pinnacle at 36 m (118 ft). The main attractions are along the ridge where due to the currents the density of shoaling fish is high and includes dogtooth tuna, barracuda, bigeye trevally, giant trevally, rainbow runners, grey reef sharks, whitetip reef sharks and eagle rays as well as normal reef species. Sometimes fierce multi-directional currents prevent all but the most experienced divers from venturing here.

ANGEL'S WINDOW

Different from the usual Lembeh diving experience, Angel's Window is a submerged pinnacle off the northwest of Lembeh Island that rises from 28 m (92 ft) to within 3 m (10 ft) of the surface. The pinnacle has several swim-throughs at about 25 m (82 ft) with a gorgonian sea fan that has several pygmy sea horses around it. All around the pinnacle there are anthias, damselfish, batfish and leaf scorpionfish and shoals of angelfish while the top often has stonefish covered in algal growth for camouflage. Visibility is usually good and trevallies and snappers are common.

The topography of the site allows divers to spiral down and up again and as they work their way down they pass colourful soft corals. Near the base of the pinnacle there are sponges and gorgonian sea fans harbouring pygmy sea horses. Throughout the site there are plenty of crinoids and nudibranchs.

TELUK KAMBAHU

Named after the village in the bay these are two more similar sites on black sand sloping from 3 m (10 ft) to 25 m (82 ft). In among the rubbish there are many different species of pipefish including ornate pipefish and robust pipefish, stargazers, mandarinfish, bangai cardinalfish, giant frogfish, painted frogfish, porcelain crabs, purple commensal shrimps, jawfish, razorfish, snowflake morays, ribbon eels, devilfish and rare and sought after weedy scorpionfish. There is a large variety of nudibranchs.

NUDI FALLS

A popular site, Nudi Falls is a small wall from 3 m (10 ft) to 28 m (92 ft) that drops to a sand and rubble slope with flying gurnards, frogfish, lionfish, mantis shrimps and pipefish. This site is well known for a variety of nudibranchs, weedy scorpionfish and pygmy sea horses.

POLICE PIER

Popular as a night dive Police Pier is another real muck dive on a sandy slope from 3 m (10 ft) to 25 m (82 ft). The bottom is covered with patches of sponges and rubble that conceal thorny sea horses, frogfish, harlequin shrimps, decorator crabs, hermit crabs, spider crabs and coral crabs. The fish life also includes snake eels, stargazers, dragonets, moray eels, octopuses and flamboyant cuttlefish. Barramundi cod and bangai cardinalfish are found in the water column. Divers have found waspfish under the pier.

FACTS

CLIMATE
Temperatures 29-32°C (84-90°F)

SEASONALITY
The sheltered conditions of the Lembeh Strait means all year round diving with the greatest number of critters being found in August. The drier season is from April to November when the wind blows from the southeast and the sea stays relatively calm. The wetter season is from December to March with cooler winds from the northwest and this can bring heavier rains and rougher seas in February. Lembeh does not get heavy monsoon rains.

GETTING THERE
Fly to Manado in the far north east of Sulawesi. There are international flights from Singapore with Silk Air and the low cost carrier Air Asia from Kuala Lumpur in Malaysia. There are also flights from Jakarta and Bali. Then travel 45 km (28 miles)-east of Manado (1.5 hours), by road.

WATER TEMPERATURE
24-29°C (75-84°F).

QUALITY OF MARINE LIFE
Very good, a high density of the weird and unusual.

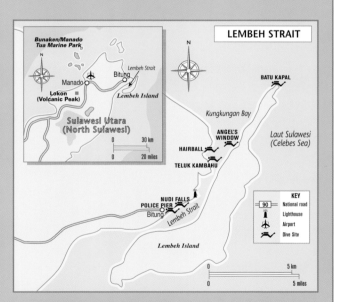

DEPTH OF DIVES
From the surface to 36 m (118 ft).

SAFETY
Currents are mostly gentle but can be fierce on spring tides.

MUCK DIVING, INDONESIA

WWII WRECKS
MICRONESIA

The State of Chuuk, known as Truk or Hogoleu before 1986, is composed of seven major island groups lying within the Eastern Caroline Islands 1,000 km (621 miles) southeast of Guam, 1,200 km (746 miles) north of Papua New Guinea.

Part of the Federated States of Micronesia, the Islands are encircled by 69 sand and coral islets giving a sheltered lagoon 65 km (40 miles) in diameter, covering an area of 2,129 square km (822 square miles).

A main naval and air base for the Japanese in the central Pacific during World War II, on February 17th and 18th 1944 an American carrier-based aerial attack sank over 60 Japanese vessels and hundreds of aircraft. The 'Ghost Fleet of Truk Lagoon' has since become a magnet for wreck divers.

Today, Chuuk (Truk) lagoon contains the remains of these Japanese ships, mostly still full of their original cargo and the personal effects of their crews.

The combination of warm water and tidal currents has transformed once proud warships into wonderful artificial reefs. Some of the wrecks are too deep for conventional diving on air but most are accessible to divers of all standards. Remember that all of these wrecks contain human remains and these should be treated with respect.

In Japanese, *maru* refers to the round trip which commercial vessels are expected to complete and it designates the name of the vessel.

FUJIKAWA MARU

One of the signature wrecks of Truk Lagoon, the *Fujikawa Maru* was a 6,938 tons, 132 m (433 ft)-long, 18 m (58 ft)-beam, armed passenger/freighter. She sits upright on the bottom. The bridge is at 15 m (49 ft), the deck at 18 m (59 ft) and keel at 35 m (115 ft). The vessel took several hits from both bombs and torpedoes and fire gutted the vessel's interior before it sank. This is one of the most beautiful wrecks in Truk Lagoon and it requires several dives to cover everything. The coral growth on the bow, derricks and mast is lush and she carries various types of ordnance, fighter aircraft bodies, aircraft engines and spare parts, Dai Nippon Beer bottles, ceramic electrical parts, shoes, uniforms and gas masks. Divers can penetrate to the baths, staterooms, galley, engine room and machine shop.

SHINKOKU MARU

Another of the best wrecks in Truk Lagoon, the *Shinkoku Maru* was 10,020 tons, 165 m (541 ft)-long and 20 m (65 ft)-beam. She was sunk by a torpedo and now sits upright in 40 m (131 ft) of water. Draped in soft corals and harbouring large shoals of glassfish, there are large guns fore and aft. The gun at the bow and the top of bridge are at 12 m (39 ft) and there are lots of personal belongings. Divers can reach an operating room and there are typewriters, telephones and 78 rpm vinyl records. Due to her size the *Shinkoku Maru* requires several dives to cover properly. This is a good wreck for night diving.

NIPPO MARU

The 3,764 tons, 106 m (348 ft)-long, 15 m (50 ft)-beam *Nippo Maru* was built in 1936. First found by Jacques-Yves Cousteau's team in 1969 she was then 'lost' until rediscovered on June 16th 1980 by Klaus Lindemann.

Another great dive, today, she sits on the bottom in

Right The WWII Japanese shipwreck *Fujikawa Maru* in Truk Lagoon
Overpage The engine room of the Shinkoku Maru, Truk lagoon

PACIFIC OCEAN

good condition with a slight list to port, the bow is at 24 m (79 ft) and the stern 44 m (144 ft). There is a torpedo hole in the port engine room and there are lots of artefacts including large guns that were both the ship's armament and cargo, other ordnance, water tanks, gas masks, bottles, barrels, electric motors and wiring, a battle tank, trucks, spare anchors, medicine boxes, radio equipment and personal effects. The battle tank is at 35 m (115 ft) and the bridge is very photogenic.

SAN FRANCISCO MARU

This is one of the most photographed wrecks in Truk because of three tanks on the deck against the bridge. The 5,831 tons, 117 m (384 ft)-long freighter *San*

Francisco Maru was built in 1919 by Kawasaki Shipyards in Kobe for Y.K. Lines (probably Nippon Yusen Kaisha). Requisitioned for the Japanese Imperial navy, she was attacked repeatedly, caught fire and sunk on an even keel in 65 m (213 ft) of water. The locals refer to her as the 'Million Dollar Wreck' both for the assortment of her cargo of war supplies and their probable monetary value.

Located in 1973, she requires several dives to do her justice. At roughly 45 m (158 ft) to the deck, 52 m (171 ft) to the stern and 58 m (190 ft) to the bottom of the forward hold, the wreck is fairly intact, there is not as much coral growth as on other wrecks but the ship is out of salvage range for most of the locals. Penetration is possible but be careful of the depth.

Left The ship's telegraph of the *Fujikawa Maru* in Truk lagoon

FACTS

CLIMATE
Tropical; dry season (the best time to travel) is between December and April; rainy season, April to December.
Typhoon season is between August and December but Chuuk (Truk) rarely gets a direct hit from a typhoon. Temperatures 27-32°C (80-90°F).

SEASONALITY
All-year-round, although photographers prefer Jan-April.

GETTING THERE
Continental Airlines with routings through Guam, Hawaii and Palau or from Europe through Manila.

WATER TEMPERATURE
Ranges between 27-29°C (80–84°F)

QUALITY OF MARINE LIFE
A high density of invertebrates, shoaling fish and larger pelagics. Stony and soft corals drape the wrecks.

DEPTH OF DIVES
From the surface to deeper than recreational divers can dive on air. The best wrecks are in 21 m (69 ft) or less but there are deeper wrecks for more advanced and technical divers.

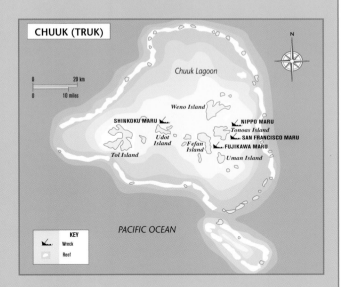

SAFETY
The level of experience required by the diver depends on the site. Deep wrecks and the penetration of wrecks should only be attempted by divers properly qualified to do so.

MANTA RAYS
MICRONESIA

Known as Wa'ab to the local people, Yap is located in the Western Caroline Islands. One of the four States that make up the Federated States of Micronesia, it is 885 km (550 miles) southwest of Guam, 579 km (360 miles) northeast of Palau and approximately 966 km (600 miles) east of the Philippines.

Yap State consists of 134 islands and atolls of which 22 are populated, stretching across more than 259,000 sq km (100,000 sq miles) of the Pacific Ocean.

The main island of Yap is made up of a cluster of four islands. The outer islands stretch nearly 966 km (600 miles) east and are sparsely populated coral atolls where the people are different from the Yapese in culture and language. The main island's four islands are very close together and joined within a common coral reef. An outer barrier reef surrounds the islands, enclosing a lagoon between the fringing reefs and the barrier reef.

Yap is famous for its clear waters and abundant reef fish and is known internationally as one of the best diving destinations to get close to manta rays.

Manta rays can be large but they are harmless plankton-feeders so they are not dangerous if approaching people out of curiosity or when being cleaned. Some mantas appear to enjoy tactile stimulation including that from divers' exhaust bubbles, they have even been known to solicit divers attention and on occasions divers have been accepted as cleaner fish when removing fishing nets or hawsers that are caught around the animal.

Around the world divers usually find manta rays near the surface or in the mid-water of lagoons or shallow reefs, particularly near to surge channels. They congregate in areas where there is rich feeding, including plankton attracted by lights at night. Feeding mantas often swim in slow vertical loops (somersaults), which they repeat over and over again.

The main island of Yap has two surge channels through opposite sides of the fringing reef between the shallow lagoon that surrounds the island and the open Pacific Ocean beyond. These concentrate the plankton and this, combined with the prevalent weather pattern, allow diving with Yap's resident population of manta rays all year round.

Right Manta rays circle in the Mi'l Channel

A NEW SPECIES OF MANTA RAY IDENTIFIED.

After five years of study a marine biologist has confirmed that a larger and migratory manta ray is in fact a distinct species. Until now it was thought that there was only one manta ray species worldwide.

Andrea Marshall, a PhD marine biologist sponsored by the Save Our Seas Foundation (SOSF), studied rays in southern Mozambique and realized that there were two distinct manta ray populations. Subsequent analysis has confirmed that these groups are in fact two distinct species. Further research has revealed that both species are present across the globe.

The new species of manta ray has large triangular pectoral fins that can span nearly 8 m (26 ft) and can weigh more than 2,000 kg (4409 lb). Unlike the more normally encountered manta ray, this one swims away from divers rather than seeking interaction. The larger manta rays are migratory so in the open ocean they are often victims of bycatch.

In the winter, when the trade winds pick up from December to April, the manta rays stay on the northwest of Yap, being cleaned by cleaner wrasse, angelfish and butterflyfish at cleaning stations in Mi'l Channel. During this season, divers may have the opportunity to observe the mantas' mating behaviour; males perform spectacular mating displays of aquabatics for females and groups of 12 or more animals swim in single file, males touching females' tails, and eventually mating belly to belly. However, due to the strong winds and rough water, most of the dive sites on the east coast will not be divable at this time. In the summer when the winds are moderate (usually from May to October), the mantas move to the Goofnuw Channel and the Valley of the Rays in the northeast of Yap. Here the manta rays are less

engaged in cleaning activity so they move around more and the divers can get away from each other.

Depending on the season, shoals of manta rays come in to these channels almost every morning as the tides turn so these dives are dependent on the tide both for getting to the sites over the shallow lagoon and for finding the best visibility.

The mantas swoop in, then hang suspended over the cleaning stations for a few minutes of grooming before swooping off again to let other mantas take their place. Where there is more than one cleaning station, each animal has its own favourite spot.

MI'L CHANNEL
Yap's best known dive site, Mi'l Channel cuts through the barrier reef on the northwest side of the Yap. Within

Below Aerial view of the Mi'l Channel, a favourite spot for mating manta rays

the channel the depth varies from 15-30 m (49-98 ft) and the area where the cleaning stations are located is about 15 m (49 ft) deep.

GOOFNUW CHANNEL – VALLEY OF THE RAYS
In the summer months the manta rays congregate on the eastern side of the reef and are cleaned in the Valley of the Rays – a section of Goofnuw Channel.

The Goofnuw channel's sandy seabed is 15-22 m (49-72 ft) deep with coral outcrops dotted about that act as cleaning stations. The largest outcrop is a lettuce coral formation locally named the Merry-Go-Round because mantas regularly circle round it. A smaller lettuce coral formation on the northern side of the channel is called the Carwash and 18 m (60 ft) from Carwash another is called Manta Rock. Both Carwash and Manta Rock rise to within 10 m (33 ft) of the surface and are good places for divers to shelter if the current is strong.

In 2008 the Yap's legislature passed a law protecting the mantas' habitat around Yap out to 19 km (12 miles) offshore.

FACTS

CLIMATE
Tropical, hot and humid. There is less rain when the northeast trade winds are blowing from November to May. Typhoons are not common but are possible. Temperatures are 26-32°C (80-90°F).

SEASONALITY
All year round but the best time to travel is between December and April.

GETTING THERE
There are regular flights by Continental Air Micronesia through Guam or Manila (Philippines).

WATER TEMPERATURE
27-29°C (80-84°F).

QUALITY OF MARINE LIFE
Extremely good, Yap is not far from the area of the greatest diversity of marine species on Earth.

DEPTH OF DIVES
Averages 15 m (49 ft) in the channels.

SAFETY
The manta rays in the channels are concentrating on being cleaned, and as long as they are left alone they will treat divers as just another harmless marine animal. Don't ride or touch them in any way, as well as causing stress this removes a protective mucous from their bodies leaving them open to infection.

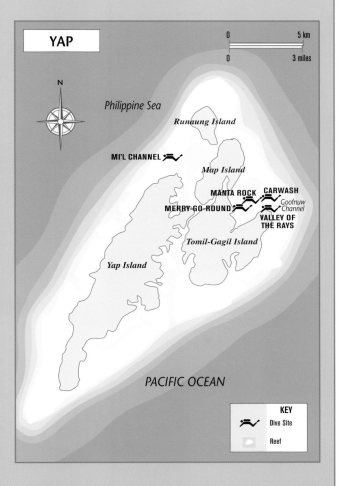

YAP

0   5 km
0   3 miles

N

Philippine Sea

Runaung Island

MI'L CHANNEL

Map Island

MANTA ROCK   CARWASH
MERRY-GO-ROUND   Goofnuw Channel
VALLEY OF THE RAYS

Tomil-Gagil Island

Yap Island

PACIFIC OCEAN

KEY
Dive Site
Reef

BLUE CORNER & JELLYFISH LAKE
MICRONESIA

The Republic of Palau, which in Palauan is *Beluu er a Belau*, is a 643 km (400 mile)-long archipelago in the Pacific Ocean that harbours one of the world's greatest concentrations of marine life.

Located between Guam, the Philippines and Papua New Guinea, Palau is 1,308 km (8l3 miles) south of Guam and 853 km (530 miles) east of the Philippines. It consists of 250 volcanic islands and a few coral atolls, but only eight islands are permanently inhabited. The Palau archipelago stretches over 241 km (l50 miles) and has 487 sq km (188 sq miles) of dry land.

The lagoon is encircled by a barrier reef that serves as a natural barrier from large Pacific swells. For divers, Palau is known for very strong currents, magnificent wall diving and brackish inland lakes populated with jellyfish.

BLUE CORNER
On spring tides, some dive sites have currents that almost rip divers' masks off. These currents are only felt when hanging on to a reef, not when drifting free with the currents. In Palau there are generally four tidal changes in a day and diving is planned around them.

At Blue Corner, the currents may be so strong that divers can be swept off the reef. Some divers overcome this by using a reef hook.

Blue corner points out into the Philippine Sea. When currents hit the wall, nutrient-rich water is forced upwards providing food that attracts smaller fish and these in turn attract larger predators. To start the dive, divers quickly descend 30 m (98 ft) into the lee of a wall that drops to over 300 m (984 ft). Still in some current, they swim along it to the reef's western edge. Shortly before a sharp bend in the wall called The Corner, there is an indent in the wall, which in strong currents can feature an upwelling referred to as The Elevator. If divers get caught in this upwelling, there is little chance of them being able to get their reef hooks attached on top of the reef.

When the dive guide finds the correct place, the divers rise to the top of the wall where they have about 5 seconds to find a dead area of coral to hook onto, otherwise the current sweeps them off the reef and they miss the fish action. Once safely attached, divers can watch the show pass by, huge humphead (Napoleon) wrasse approach closely and the reef top harbours redtooth triggerfish, moorish idols, fusiliers, turtles, angelfish and butterflyfish. Off the wall, blacktip reef, grey reef and whitetip reef sharks prey on shoals of barracuda, surgeonfish, snappers and jacks.

Many divers are soon low on air so the dive guide signals for all the divers to unhook at the same time. Swept off the reef the divers slowly ascend to 5 m (16 ft) for a safety stop where the dive guide deploys a safety sausage, buoy or flag surface marker buoy (SMB) to alert the dive boat. Truly an electrifying dive.

JELLYFISH LAKE
Located on Mecherchar Island, (formerly Eil Malk Island), 29 km (18 miles) from Koror, snorkelling in Jellyfish Lake is a most unusual experience. Full of surprising numbers of golden jellyfish, *Mastigias papua etpisoni,* a subspecies of *Mastigias papua*, the lake is a major tourist attraction. The lake also has moon jellyfish (*Aurelia* sp.), who spend most daylight hours in deepwater so they are not obvious.

Jellyfish Lake, (*Ongeim'l Tketau* in Palauan), is one of approximately 70 brackish lakes scattered throughout the limestone Rock Islands of Palau. After purchasing a

Right Silhouette of a mastigias jellyfish, Jellyfish Lake

The island of Kakaban in Indonesia and several islands in Palau have land-locked, brackish lakes containing Mastigias jellyfish. The sting of the Mastigias is mild and often undetectable, but snorkellers may feel their sting on sensitive skin, such as the area around their mouth.

Over 35 million years ago, colliding tectonic plates caused the massive Pacific plate to slide under and lift the Philippine plate. Since its uplift, the exposed seabed has been eaten away by a variety of erosive forces. As rain falls it absorbs CO_2 from the atmosphere making it acidic synthesizes various humic acids from mixing with decaying vegetation. These weak acids slowly ate away at the limestone rock. As rising oceans and incoming tides carried percolating sea water through fissures into the lakes, they also carried the larvae of a variety of invertebrate organisms and fish including moon jellyfish and golden jellyfish (*Mastigias papua*). Over the years the Mastigias jellyfish developed into separate subspecies of Mastigias papua depending on the lake concerned and five subspecies have been named in honour of five elected Presidents of Palau.

The Mastigias jellyfish feed by capturing small zooplankton with their nematocysts (stinging cells) but trapped inside the lake they did not find enough plankton to support them. Fortunately, like many stony corals they have symbiotic zooxanthellae, algae that collect sunlight and photosynthesize, creating an excess of sugars and proteins to feed the jellyfish during the day. They migrate across the lakes following the sun during the day and sink to the bottom to collect nitrates and phosphates to fertilize their algae after dark.

There are two main types of brackish lake on Palau: mixed and stratified. With mixed lakes, temperature, salinity, and the amount of dissolved oxygen hardly change with depth. However, with stratified lakes, due to limited water movement the deeper water lacks oxygen (anoxic) and has high concentrations of hydrogen sulphide below the thermocline. Most jellyfish lakes are stratified with the oxygen-less lower layer starting at 12–14 m (39–46 ft) and marked by a pink bacterial layer about 1 m (39 inches)-thick.

It is thought that migration across the lake is partly due to predation by the sea anemone *Entacmea medusivora*. This anemone is found at the side of the lakes and migrating east in the morning and west in the afternoon ensures the jellyfish always encounter a shadow before the actual side of the lake. Keeping out of the shadows keeps them away from the edge where this predator is found. The jellyfish's avoidance of shadows also causes them to form dense aggregations at the illuminated edge of the shadow.

Two lakes at Palau are referred to as Jellyfish Lake, one on Mercherchar Island and one on Koror Island. Visiting divers are only allowed access to the Jellyfish Lake (Officially known as Ongeim'l Tketau) on the island of Mercherchar (formally referred to as Eil Malk Island). Due to a substantial increase in temperature initiated by the 1997–98 El Niño/Southern Oscillation (ENSO), and the period of cool water – La Niña – which followed it, by December 1998 the golden jellyfish in this lake had suffered a 90% decline in numbers. An agreement was made with the dive centres to put Jellyfish Lake off-limits in the hope that the jellyfish would recover. The Mastigias jellyfish have two separate life stages, the free-swimming jellyfish and the tiny bottom-dwelling asexual solitary polyp. This asexual larva form lived at the bottom of the lake and feeds on microscopic copepods until the water cools down, then slowly buds off new young medusa to complete the life cycle and bring the population of Mastigias jellyfish back to normal. The warmer water did not affect the moon jellyfish which continued to thrive.

Left Close-up of a golden jellyfish (*Mastigias papua*).

permit, visitors access the lake by a short trail over a ridge, which separates the lake from the surrounding lagoon. The walk in has rope guides in some places and signs to provide an introduction to the flora and fauna of the rainforest en route.

Eventually visitors reach a slippery, wooden jetty at the northwest corner of the lake and can then snorkel out into the lake.

A fragile environment, diving and using fins are banned to avoid disturbing the toxic hydrogen sulphide layer and damage to the jellyfish, and because exhaled gases can become trapped in tissue pockets of the jellyfishs' bell, lifting them to the surface and tearing delicate tissue. Snorkellers should wear lifejackets to help avoid stirring up the hydrogen sulphide layer, should not kick among the jellyfish, should remain in a prone position on the surface and propel themselves with gentle strokes. They should also make sure to carry environmentally-clean equipment, check their pockets for any organic materials and not apply sunscreen before entering the water.

During daylight, golden jellyfish are found in spectacular aggregations along the illuminated edges of shadows cast by the mangroves that line the lake's shore. Avoiding the shadows helps them to avoid the predatory sea anemones (*Entacmea medusivora*) as well as remaining in the sun for photosynthesis.

Before dawn, millions of golden jellyfish mill around

Below Snorkeler surrounded by jellyfish in Jellyfish Lake

the western half of the lake, swimming in all directions. When the sky brightens in the east, the jellyfish swim towards the sun until they reach the shadows at the eastern end of the lake where they they know that predatory sea anemones reside.

In the afternoon, as the sun begins to travel westward, the jellyfish accumulated in the east of the lake begin to follow the sun back across the surface, returning to where they started in the morning. The jellyfish swim west until they reach the shadow along the western edge of the lake, where they accumulate, remaining in the sunlight to avoid the shore.

By late afternoon all the jellyfish return to the western end of the lake. As the sun sets the animals begin to swim vertically, up and down in the water column. This behaviour keeps them away from the shore.

FACTS

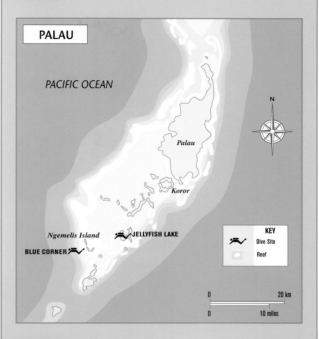

CLIMATE
Tropical, warm and humid with frequent showers. Average temperature 27°C (81°F). Wet season May to November.

SEASONALITY
Best time to go: October till early June.

GETTING THERE
International flights to Koror with Continental Micronesia via Guam or Manila.

WATER TEMPERATURE
Averages 27-29°C (80-84°F).

QUALITY OF MARINE LIFE
Diverse and prolific at Blue Corner. Many jellyfish in the lake.

DEPTH OF DIVES
30 m (98 ft), it is possible to go deeper than sport divers should dive on air at Blue Corner. Stay at the surface in Jellyfish Lake.

SAFETY
Currents are strong and can be fierce at Blue Corner. There are no particular safely issues in Jellyfish Lake

THE GREAT BARRIER REEF
AUSTRALIA

Stretching in roughly a northwest-southeast direction from Papua New Guinea in the north, to Lady Elliott Island off Bundaberg in Queensland in the south, The Great Barrier Reef is the largest coral reef system on Earth.

It is not one continuous, unbroken reef, but a complex of coral reefs, shoals, islets and cays off the northeastern coast of Australia. It can be seen from outer space and is the world's largest single structure made by living organisms.

Located in the Coral Sea off the coast of Queensland, the Great Barrier Reef is separated from the Australian mainland by a shallow stretch of water 15–160 km (9–99 miles)-wide and consists of over 2,900 individual reefs and 900 islands stretching for 2,600 km (1,616 miles). The total area is approximately 344,470 sq km (133,000 sq miles).

COD HOLE

Cod Hole is a sheltered reef where fishermen used to clean their catch. Northeast of Cape Flattery and east-northeast of Lizard Island, it is 150 km (93 miles) north of Cairns. Moorings for boats are limited. First made famous by Ron and Valerie Taylor due to the large, well-fed potato cod, humphead (Napoleon or Maori) wrasse and moray eels, divemasters now regularly feed the fish, and the larger ones can be boisterous. Potato cod, *Epinephelus tukula* (also called potato rockcod, potato grouper or potato bass, can reach a length of 2 m (6.5 ft) and Humphead wrasse 2.3 m (7.5 ft).

One of the world's best-known dive sites, Cod Hole is roughly 24 km (15 miles) from the upmarket resort of Lizard Island. Divers find that the corals vary from plate corals to isolated pinnacles to walls and channels, canyons and shallow soft coral gardens. The depth is from 5-30 m (16-98 ft), and there are large shoals of fish due to the regular feeding including angelfish and butterflyfish and coral trout, plus anemones, giant clams and whitetip and grey reef sharks.

Right A shoal of fish flee a diver at cod hole

Overpage A humphead wrasse looms in waters around Cod Hole

HUMPHEAD WRASSE (GIANT WRASSE/NAPOLEON WRASSE)

Wrasse are the most diverse of fishes, with some 300 species, ranging from the 2 cm (3/4 inch) (*Minilabrus striatus*) to the immense humphead (Napoleon) wrasse (*Cheilinus undulatus*), which have been caught 2.3 m (7 ft) long, weighing 190 kg (418 lb).

Wrasse are usually brightly coloured and often change colour, and from female to male as they grow from juvenile through the intermediate phase to terminal phase. Once sex reversal occurs, males set up territories and maintain a harem of females.

Humphead wrasse are diurnal: hiding in caves and hollows at night. Blue-green in colour, they darken with age. Terminal males develop a pronounced hump on their foreheads. They are carnivorous, having prominent canine teeth adapted to pull molluscs off rocks or seize crustaceans, urchins and other invertebrates, which are then crushed with their pharyngeal teeth. At the moment of predation, the jaw is extended forward, catching out many divers, who find themselves scarred after illegally feeding eggs to them!

Humphead (Napoleon) wrasse are popular eating but research shows that larger specimens have often accumulated more natural mercury in their bodies than is considered safe for human consumption.

SS YONGALA

Australia's best wreck dive, often called the *Titanic* of Townsville, the SS *Yongala* sailed into a cyclone and sank in 1911. In 1976 she was protected under Australia's Historic Shipwrecks Act, and special permits are required to dive the wreck and nothing can be disturbed within a 500 m (1,640 ft) radius.

Today she is one of Australia's best dive sites, lying on her starboard side in 27 m (89 ft) of water with her port side at 12 m (39 ft), the bow is the deepest point and is pointing 347°. The hull is mostly intact. The only shelter in a large expanse of sea, she has become an attraction for an amazing variety of marine life including enormous fish. Easily found due to the fixed moorings,

Below A potato cod emerges from the SS *Yongala* wreck

penetrating the vessel and interference with artefacts is prohibited. Divers need to treat the vessel as several dives; it is wise to descend the mooring line until one is in the lee of the wreck and then be careful not to be swept off into open water. There are some human remains, crockery, cutlery, lamps, toilets and baths and the hull is covered with soft and stony corals, sponges, gorgonian sea fans and sea whips, but it is the fish that catches one's attention.

Shoals of batfish, jacks, rainbow runners, snappers, barracuda, soldierfish and cobia appear to come out to greet divers. Stingrays jostle for position as they search out food, eagle rays, humphead (Napoleon or Maori) wrasse, coral trout, moray eels, sea snakes and wobbegongs are common while reef sharks, guitar sharks and turtles may be seen. Watch out for enormous Queensland Groupers who can be aggressive.

The phenomenal fish population and luxuriant marine growth are the result of strong currents that can be a challenge and surface conditions can be too rough for diving.

FACTS

CLIMATE
Temperatures 24-28°C (75–82°F) but cooler at sea. Cyclone season is January through March but December is also usually rough too.

SEASONALITY
Best October to June. Avoid the months of possible cyclones.

GETTING THERE
For Cod Hole travel to Cairns or Port Douglas and board a live-aboard boat. For the SS *Yongala* fly or drive to Townsville.

WATER TEMPERATURE
22–27°C (72–80°F).

QUALITY OF MARINE LIFE
Exceptional, abundant and the fish are unusually large.

DEPTH OF DIVES
Maximum 30 m (98 ft).

SAFETY
Currents are often strong and can be fierce. The Yongala is suitable for all levels of diver so long as the currents are not too strong.

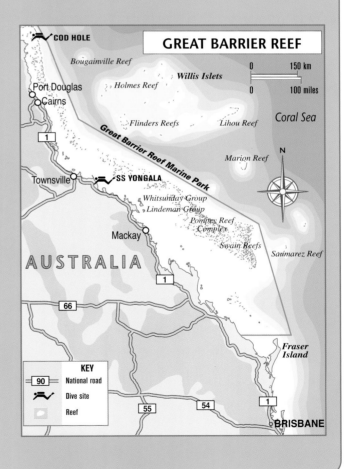

GREAT BARRIER REEF

Bougainville Reef
Willis Islets
Holmes Reef
Port Douglas
Cairns
Flinders Reefs
Lihou Reef
Coral Sea
Great Barrier Reef Marine Park
Marion Reef
Townsville
SS YONGALA
Whitsunday Group
Lindeman Group
Pompey Reef Complex
Mackay
Swain Reefs
Saumarez Reef
AUSTRALIA
Fraser Island
BRISBANE

KEY
90 — National road
Dive site
Reef

AIRCRAFT WRECKS
PAPUA NEW GUINEA

Milne Bay (or 'Millen Bay' as the locals pronounce it) is the easternmost inlet on the coast at the southeastern tip of the Papua New Guinean mainland. It has a variety of diving attractions including pristine coral reefs, underwater volcanic vents, caves and various species of fish including manta rays, many colourful tropical fish, whales and dolphins.

Ascene of heavy fighting during World War II, the region is littered with shipwrecks and aircraft wrecks. Milne Bay is a deep natural harbour 10 km (6 miles)-wide and 31 km (19 miles)-long.

The quietist province in Papua New Guinea (PNG), Milne Bay is hard to get to – there is little in the way of road links to other provinces, and not much in the way of inward passenger shipping.

Live-aboard dive boats offer the most extensive coverage of diving in the Milne Bay region but there are resorts on land. The variety of marine life is vast. There are rare scorpionfish like Merlet's scorpionfish (*Rhinopias aphanes*) but divers will also find creatures that have not yet been recorded from other places of the world, soft and stony corals, manta ray cleaning stations and great muck diving.

LOCKHEED P-38 LIGHTNING FIGHTER AIRCRAFT

Other P-38 wrecks are known in this area, but in September 2004, Bob and Dinah Halstead were talking to friends at Boga Boga village on Cape Vogel when they were told to visit Henry Katura from Magabara village because he had seen the wreck of an aircraft when out on a reef fishing for sea cucumbers (bêche-de-mer).

With the help of Henry's father Remigus, Bob, Dinah and some others located the aircraft resting on the reef slope completely intact from 12-17 m (30-56 ft). 12 m (37 ft 10 inches)-long and with a wingspan of 16 m (52 ft), the growth of corals and sponges on the aircraft wreck was significant.

Rugged, fast and versatile, the American P-38 Lightning shot down more Japanese aircraft than any other. The armament consisted of four 12.7 mm (0.50-in) machine guns and one 20 mm (0.787 inch) cannon, all housed in the nose section directly ahead of the pilot's cockpit. These and the cockpit's gauges are visible in the wreck.

Research showed that the aircraft was shipped to the 5th USAAF in Australia on 12th August 1942 from San Francisco and was lost four months later on a delivery flight to Milne Bay. Flown by Richard Chello, the aircraft suffered engine failure and had to be ditched. The pilot was rescued.

BOEING B-17 FLYING FORTRESS BOMBER – BLACKJACK

In 1986, Rodney Pearce, accompanied by David Pennefather and Bruce Johnson, were searching for an aircraft wreck near Cape Vogel when local villagers said that there was a 4-engined aircraft wreck just off the beach. A B-17F-20-BO Flying Fortress bomber was lying on a sandy bottom in 46 m (151 ft) of water near the village of Boga Boga. This wreck, now famous as Blackjack, is one of the top aircraft wrecks in the world.

The area's best known dive site, the aircraft had the serial number 41-24521 and, as the last two digits were 21, it was given the nickname 'Blackjack' after the card game of the same name.

Right The tail of the wrecked Boeing B-17 bomber 'Blackjack', Milne Bay

Piloted by Lt. Ralph DeLoach on its final mission in 1943, it took off from Port Moresby to attack Rabaul. Problems developed with the engines on the right wing but the bombs were dropped over the target. On the return home they could not hold a straight course and got lost. The Co-Pilot, Lt Joseph H. Moore, had previously ditched a bomber so DeLoach handed the controls to him and he ditched near Boga Boga village on 11th July 1943, 22 km (12 nautical miles) east of the P-38F-5-LO Lightning 42-12649.

Three of the crew of ten were injured but helped by villagers, and all of the crew survived.

The Flying Fortress was a big bomber. Powered by four Wright R-18200-97 Cyclone radial engines, each producing 1,200 hp, it was 23 m (74 ft 4 inches)-long, with a wingspan of 32 m (103 ft 9 inches). Thirteen machine guns protected the crew, hence the name Flying Fortress.

The aircraft hit the sand but bounced back into the upright position, her dented nose pointing away from the reef wall. The visibility allows divers to see all that remains of the aircraft as they descend the face of the reef. It has some soft coral and sponge growth. The four propellers are intact and ammunition can still be seen in the gun turrets. By today's standards this is a deep dive if performed on air, but those suitably trained can perform decompression stops along the reef observing the many reef creatures.

Left Coral growth on the gun turret of the wrecked Boeing B-17 bomber 'Blackjack', Milne Bay

FACTS

CLIMATE
Tropical, southeast trade winds blow from May to November. Rainfall is variable with no well-defined wet season. Cyclones are rare.

SEASONALITY
October to June avoids strongest southeast trade winds. October to December generally enjoy the best and most consistent weather while January to March usually experience strong south-easterly winds.

GETTING THERE
Air Niugini flies to Port Moresby from Sydney, Brisbane, Cairns, Singapore and Manila and there are Air Niugini connecting flights from Port Moresby to Alotau's airport Gurney on most days of the week.

WATER TEMPERATURE
Variable but are usually in range from 27°C (80°F) in July/August to 29°C (84°F) in December/January.

QUALITY OF MARINE LIFE
Very good, a high density of stony and soft corals, gorgonias, other invertebrates and both reef and pelagic fish including sharks.

DEPTH OF DIVES
Maximum 46 m (151 ft).

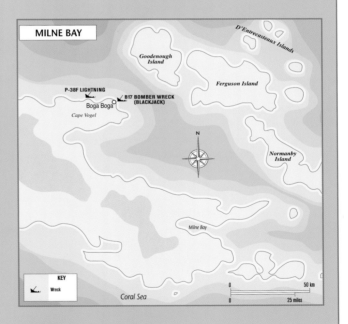

SAFETY
Currents are mild. Blackjack is a decompression dive so decompression stops are essential.

KELP FORESTS

USA

Santa Catalina Island, often referred to as Catalina Island, or just Catalina, is a rocky island 35 km (22 miles) south-southwest of Los Angeles off the coast of the American state of California.

The island is 35 km (22 miles)-long and 13 km (8 miles)-wide at its widest point and has an area of 194 sq km (75 sq miles). The island narrows to 800 m (half of a mile)-wide at the isthmus between two harbours in the northwest part of the island.

Due to the cold, clear water and plenty of sunlight, the sea is dominated by kelp, particularly giant kelp and its associated fauna. Divers play hide and seek among the forest with fish such as garibaldi damselfish, yellowtail, also called amberjack, (*Seriola lalandi*), calico (kelp) bass, white sea bass, giant sea bass and many more.

Giant kelp (*Macrocystis pyrifera*) may grow 0.5 m (20 inches) in a day and individual plants can rise to the surface from 30 m (98 ft). Giant kelp requires a rocky seabed, and holdfasts anchor the plants to large rocks and once the plant reaches the surface, it continues to grow horizontally, forming a canopy.

The plant has a stem-like stipe from which long leaf-like fronds known as blades grow. The blades have a wrinkled surface to help in photosynthesis.

ITALIAN GARDENS

Italian Gardens is a kelp forest in 25 m (82 ft) of water, where the sun penetrates the kelp canopy, making for spectacular diving. This site has large, tame black sea bass and lots of Garibaldi damselfish. Pacific angel sharks are found on the sand but divers must concentrate hard on the seabed to see them as their camouflage is very good.

CASINO POINT

The Casino Point Marine Park is less than ten minutes walk from the centre of Avalon. First established in 1964, this site has become a Mecca to divers with an abundance of marine life, giant kelp forests and several shipwrecks to explore. Artificial reefs have been established to provide additional habitats. The depth ranges from the rocky shore to 29 m (95 ft).

Because of strict local laws prohibiting the taking of game or salvaging artefacts, the park has become home for a large variety of marine life. Plant life of all colours exists, from giant kelp to the smallest algae. Living within the rocky reef are California spiny lobsters, abalone, octopuses, moray eels, tiny nudibranchs and bigger fish.

Swimming freely in the kelp forest are calico (kelp) bass, senorita fish, California sheephead, California opaleye, blacksmith and garibaldi damselfish. Where the rocky reef ends and sandy bottom begins divers may find Pacific angel sharks, California bat rays, banded guitarfish and California halibut (also called California flounder).

The dive site itself is easily accessible via a staircase leading directly to an entry platform from the walkway. Once in the water, the surf is usually calm or near calm and visibility is always quite good. The marine life is abundant and usually tame. Divers will find several small wrecks within easy swimming distance of the entry stairs.

Extending out from the Casino Point is the man-made Casino Groin or breakwater. The underwater park extends from in front of the Casino to nearly the end of the groin and out about 50 m (164 ft). The park is

Right Kelp fronds showing pneumatocysts at Santa Catalina Island

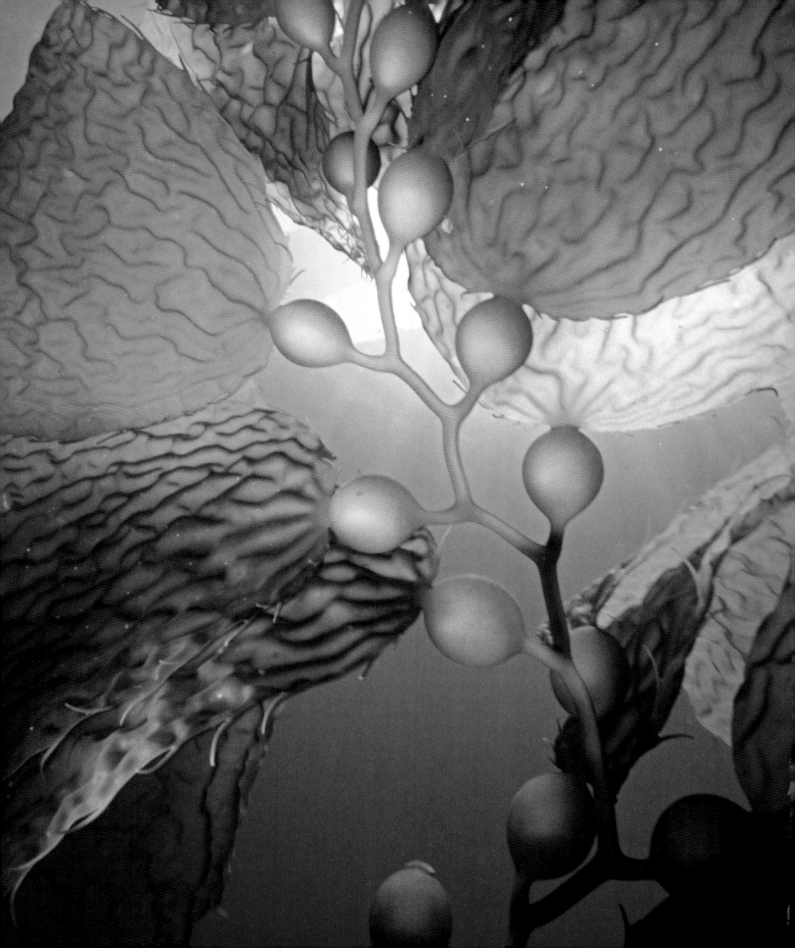

segregated with buoys and rope to keep out boat traffic. There is always a mild current.

FARNSWORTH BANK

Approximately 3 km (2 miles) west of Ben Weston Point on Catalina Island, Farnsworth Bank is the largest of a number of pinnacles rising from 61 m (200 ft) to 20 m (65 ft). One of the most popular dive sites at Catalina, the weather has to be good to be able to reach it, because it is in the open-ocean on Catalina's exposed Pacific side ('backside'). The marine life here is very rich and includes dense growths of the rare purple hydrocoral (*Allopora californica*). The diving is considered advanced due to the depth, the current, and the need to watch out for fishermen near the surface. Other sightings for divers include black sea bass and moray eels.

Left A shoal of blacksmith fish move through the kelp

FACTS

CLIMATE
Catalina has a year-round Mediterranean climate with warm, sunny days and cool evening breezes. In summer, the average temperature is 24°C (75°F) while in winter average temperature is 18°C (65°F).

SEASONALITY
The best times to dive are during the warm and dry summer months with August and September having the warmest water temperatures. However for the best deals and less crowding the off season (November 1st – April 30th) is good, the water temperatures are cooler but the diving is even more spectacular.

GETTING THERE
Fly to Los Angeles in California and then take the express ferry to Avalon, which takes around 1.5 hours.

WATER TEMPERATURE
Water temperature averages 15 to 21°C (60-70°F). Dive in a dry-suit or 7 mm (0.276 inch) semidry-suit.

QUALITY OF MARINE LIFE
Very good, giant kelp, purple hydrocorals, California sea lions, crevice kelpfish, common octopus, California spiny lobsters, black sea bass, yellowtails (amberjack, *Seriola lalandei*), barracuda, California bat rays, garibaldi damselfish and torpedo rays, leopard, horn and soupfin sharks while blue and shortfin mako sharks and sunfish are also seen in the open water.

DEPTH OF DIVES
Sites range from 10–30 m (33–98 ft) but one can go deeper than divers should on air.

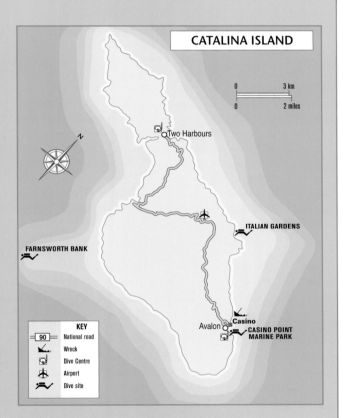

CATALINA ISLAND

Two Harbours

ITALIAN GARDENS

FARNSWORTH BANK

Avalon
Casino
CASINO POINT MARINE PARK

KEY
90 — National road
Wreck
Dive Centre
Airport
Dive site

SAFETY
Currents can be fierce on the Pacific side of the island, watch out for boat traffic on Farnsworth Banks.
Divers should be careful not to get entangled in kelp – it is common for divers to panic when they feel that they are caught up in it. You should remain still and snap the kelp off to free yourself.

KELP FORESTS, USA

El Niño conditions can lead to unusual weather patterns in some diving areas. Warmer than usual seawater causes many sharks to descend into deeper, colder water. More significantly, animals that have symbiotic algae may expel them, as happens in coral bleaching.

In years of normal weather, ocean water heated by the tropical sun is pushed by trade winds from the eastern Pacific to the western Pacific. In the western Pacific the warm water piles up to give higher sea levels around countries like Indonesia, Malaysia and the Philippines. In the eastern Pacific, in the trade-wind belts off the western coasts of America, upwelling, nutrient-rich cold water replaces the wind driven warm surface water. This leads to rich fishing off Peru and Ecuador and causes the overlying air to cool below the temperature at which water vapour condenses (the dew point), producing fog.

Around December the trade winds slacken and the Intertropical Convergence Zone, which is usually located north of the geographical equator, shifts south. The slackening trade winds cause the westward flowing current to slow, reducing the coastal upwelling in the eastern Pacific and allowing warmer water to invade the region.

Every few years, this seasonal warming is more intense and prolonged than usual, producing the oceanographic event known as El Niño, coupled with a reversal in atmospheric circulation known as the Southern Oscillation. El Niño is Spanish for 'The Boy Child', because Peruvian fishermen noticed that it often began around Christmas, and together they are called the El Niño-Southern Oscillation Phenomenon (ENSO).

When an El Niño occurs, the entire equatorial current and atmospheric circulation pattern reverses, and this brings warm water and air from the western Pacific to the Galápagos, Cocos and Malpelo Islands and coastal South America. In association with this, the normal atmospheric high-pressure system in the eastern Pacific is replaced with a low-pressure one, and the low-pressure system in the western Pacific is replaced with a high-pressure one. The warm surface water is no longer pushed west and allows a cold, nutrient-rich upwelling off the coasts of Peru and Ecuador. The warmer sea-surface temperature transforms the eastern Pacific coastal climate from arid to wet and causes the huge fish stocks normally associated with the upwelling nutrient-rich cold water to migrate away.

In the water, off the coasts of Peru and Ecuador, the fish are forced to either feed at greater depths or leave the warmer water altogether, returning only when the water cools down

again. This is noticeable to divers as the sharks at Cocos and elsewhere become less evident at diving depths.

Where the sea level has dropped, the reduced cover of water allows more heat and ultraviolet light from the sun to impinge on shallower invertebrates; this exacerbates the warmer water conditions that lead to the bleaching of many of the immobile invertebrates found in water shallower than 15 m (49 ft). Unable to move away from the warmer conditions, stony corals, sea anemones and giant clams must either weather El Niño or die. These invertebrates rely on zooxanthellae, the symbiotic algae that gives them their colour, for most of their food intake but under stress they evict it from their tissues. If conditions return to normal quickly, they may survive, and in some cases they may be able to replace the evicted zooxanthellae with another species of zooxanthellae that can survive warmer conditions. However, if the El Niño event is a long-lasting one, the bleached invertebrates will perish.

El Niño is called 'a warm event'. La Niña, meaning 'the Little Girl', also called Viejo, the Spanish for old, is a cold event. The opposite of El Niño, with unusually cold surface temperatures in the eastern Equatorial Pacific, it usually but not always follows an El Niño. The effects on global climate are the opposite to those of El Niño.

Below A bleached coral reef off the Maldives Islands

SCALLOPED HAMMERHEAD SHARKS
THE GOLDEN TRIANGLE

The Golden Triangle consists of Ecuador's Galápagos Islands and the live-aboard only destinations of Costa Rica's Cocos Island and Colombia's Malpelo Island off the west coast of Central America.

The Galápagos Islands consist of 13 major islands, 6 smaller islands and 70 islets and rocks spread over a wide area 1,000 km (620 miles) west of the mainland of Ecuador.

The Cocos and Malpelo Islands are in the Equatorial Countercurrent. Cocos Island, 418 km (260 miles) southwest of Costa Rica, is 8 km (5 miles) long and has two natural harbours on its north coast.

The Malpelo Island is 500 km (310 miles) off the western coast of Colombia, and is a bleak collection of jagged pinnacles protruding 300 m (984 ft) out of the ocean.

THE GALÁPAGOS ISLANDS

An all-round diving destination, the Galápagos Islands also have shoaling scalloped hammerhead sharks, which are most prolific around the northern islands of Wolf and Darwin.

At the most northern island, Darwin Island, The Arch is a splendid sight from the surface but even better underwater. Sitting on a plateau below the surface, the wall drops-off into the depths and is a point of focus for the fish and countless shoaling scalloped hammerhead sharks. There is a natural viewing platform at 18 m (59 ft) on the ocean side of the arch. Divers also encounter Galápagos sharks, eagle rays and green and hawksbill turtles here, but the area has no protection. Anchorage is poor, the surface can be rough and the strong currents can be unpredictable with downwellings common.

COCOS AND MALPELO ISLANDS

The diving at Cocos and Malpelo Islands is 'fish action' off sheer cliffs that plunge into deep water. These regions teem with big fish but the main interest is the shoals of hundreds of female scalloped hammerhead sharks that line up in the strong currents by day and leave to feed elsewhere at night. Even without the hammerheads, there is large-animal action: whale sharks, manta and mobula rays, packs of eagle and marbled rays and whitetip reef sharks are everywhere. Divers descend rapidly to around 15–25 m (49–82 ft), find a crevice in the rocks, wedge in and wait for the fish to approach.

At Cocos Island strong currents are common at many sites, particularly those with exciting action such as Alcyone, Dirty Rock or Manuelita Island.

Dirty Rock has massive boulders sloping down the south side and a 100 m (328 ft)-wide channel separating the main rock from a collection of pinnacles. Whitetip reef sharks are everywhere, often so densely packed that they are stacked on top of each other, but most divers come to see the large shoals of scalloped hammerhead sharks. Sometimes these sharks are encountered near to the surface but mostly they are found below the thermoclines, the majority of the diving is between 18 and 30 m (59 and 98 ft), occasionally 40 m (131 ft). Squadrons of female scalloped hammerhead sharks appear out of the blue, swim majestically by and recede into the distance to be replaced by further shoals, ten, twenty, fifty even hundreds at a time. Scalloped hammerhead sharks tend to be spooked by the noise of divers exhaust bubbles

Right A diver observes a large scalloped hammerhead shark off the Galapagos

so the live-aboard boats offer training in the use of rebreathers so that divers can get closer to the sharks. Bait-balls, dense shoals of trevallies or similar small species that are attacked by sharks, dolphins and tuna are often found, divers should be very careful around these as sharks will snatch at anything when participating in feeding frenzies.

Below A scalloped hammerhead shark on the prowl off the Cocos Islands

The dive sites at Malpelo Island are similar to those at Cocos but the seas can be wilder. Hundreds of moray eels swim around with large snappers, groupers and manta rays. The Three Musketeers, a group of pinnacles off the northern end of Malpelo, have a series of tunnels and caverns; the largest, The Cathedral, is full of fish including baitfish and whitetip reef sharks. The water

temperature below the thermoclines is illustrated by the names of other diving sites on the island's north side such as The Freezer, The Fridge and Freezer wall.

The waters here have scalloped hammerhead sharks shoaling at the surface as well as deeper down and huge shoals of silky sharks.

At all three destinations the diving is for relatively experienced divers who are used to rough surface conditions and strong currents, which can change at any time.

FACTS

CLIMATE

Galápagos: Subtropical with two seasons, the changeover between the seasons is variable. The dry, or Garua, season runs from July to December, 'Garua' refers to the fog and mist that often hangs on the higher elevations at this time, air temperatures average 26°C (80°F). The warmer or wet season, where air temperatures often exceed 30°C (86°F), lasts from January through June, with March and April generally being the wettest months.

Cocos and Malpelo: Tropical with high rainfall and two seasons, average rainfall is 2,540 mm (100 inches) at Cocos Island and 1,060 mm (42 inches) at Malpelo. At sea level air temperatures can reach 32°C (89°F). The dry season provides calmer seas for the long boat journey out to the islands and there are more Silky Sharks and Mobula Rays, there are some Scalloped Hammerhead Sharks but not the large numbers that are encountered during the rainy season.

SEASONALITY

Galápagos: The calmest waters are between December and March to April but it is also wetter. The clearest water is from October till November.

Cocos and Malpelo: November till May for the dry season, June till November for the wet season, July/August for the largest number of Hammerhead Sharks.

GETTING THERE

Galápagos: Boats depart from San Cristobal or Baltra Island, connecting flights are via Quito or Guayaquil.

Cocos and Malpelo: Fly to San Jose then for Cocos Island transfer by road to Puntarenus to pick up the live-aboard boat or for Malpelo Island fly to Golfito to pick up the live-aboard boat.

WATER TEMPERATURE

Galápagos: Warmest from January to May, 22–28°C (72–82°F) and coolest from July to November, 16–22°C (61–72°F)

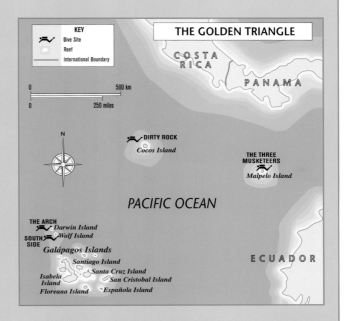

Cocos and Malpelo: 25–28°C (78–82°F) at the surface, below the thermoclines it can drop to 15°C (60°F).

QUALITY OF MARINE LIFE

The larger animals are prolific.

DEPTH OF DIVES

Galápagos: 5–24 m (15–80 ft), Cocos Island: 18–40 m (60–130 ft), Malpelo: the surface to 40 m (surface to 130 ft).

SAFETY

Currents are strong and can be fierce. These areas are best suited to advanced or strong divers.

CAVE DIVING

NEW ZEALAND

The eroded remains of a group of ancient volcanoes, the Poor Knights Islands are a group of uninhabited islands lying off the east coast of the Northland Region of New Zealand's North Island.

They are located 50 km (31 miles) to the northeast of Whangarei and are 24 km (15 miles) offshore half way between Bream Head and Cape Brett.

The group consists of two large islands, Tawhiti Rahi to the north and Aorangi to the south with a group of smaller islets, rock stacks and pinnacles with steep cliffs, which often plummet 100 m (328 ft) below sea level and offer over 100 dive sites.

The steep cliffs plunge into a marine environment that is as unique as the islands themselves: leather kelp forests, sand channels, giant sea caves, archways and underwater caverns create different habitats within a small area, the Poor Knights Islands contain more species of fish and invertebrates than can be found anywhere else in New Zealand coastal waters.

The Poor Knights Islands are one of the top scuba diving destinations in the world according to Jacques-Yves Cousteau. They offer a diversity of reef and pelagic fish and invertebrates and there are leather kelp forests (*Ecklonia radiata*) and red and green seaweed. The encrusting life on the walls is very colourful, with an abundance of soft corals, jewel anemones and bryozoans.

There are three species of ray, the eagle ray, the short-tailed stingray and the long-tailed stingray. Spotted black groupers (the only fully-protected fish in New Zealand waters), toadstool and gold ribbon groupers and Lord Howe butterflyfish are all established. Rare sightings have included manta rays, lionfish, trumpetfish and longnose butterflyfish. There are six species of moray eels, and shoals of many other species including kingfish (amberjack), two-spot demoiselles, and shoals of both pink and blue maomao, koheru and trevallies. During the summer stingrays gather in archways to mate. Sponges, anemones, gorgonias, soft corals, tunicates and nudibranchs are found in profusion.

Subtropical and temperate marine species coexist. Many of the species here have found their way to the Poor Knights Islands on the subtropical East Auckland current – a continuation of the East Australian Current along the eastern coast of New Zealand's North Island; the current is part of the western boundary current system of the South Pacific subtropical gyre.

There are several fish species present within the reserve that are absent or extremely rare in the rest of New Zealand.

RIKORIKO CAVE

Formed by a gas bubble during a volcanic eruption, on the west of Aorangi Island Rikoriko Cave is one of the world's largest sea caves at some 60 m (197 ft)-across. Large enough to allow yachts to enter, some charter-boats use it as an overnight mooring and organize night dives there.

The water at the entrance of Rikoriko cave glows with a blue light. The name Rikoriko refers to this shimmering light that reflects from the water's surface. Ferns hang from the roof receiving light for photosynthesis from the reflections off the sea and their freshwater from what percolates through the porous roof of the cave. The walls of the cave are covered in algae and patterned with colour from minerals seeping through.

Right A diver descends into Rikoriko Cave

On night dives divers find that many fish species are resting as if asleep and easy to approach. There are also some nudibranch species which are not seen during the day.

TIE DYE ARCH

Tie Dye Arch is a beautiful arch which extends from just below the surface down to 40 m (131 ft). Located at the Pinnacles, about 8 km (5 miles)-south of Aorangi Island it is very exposed so it is only accessible in flat, calm conditions. The name comes from the colourful patterns of sponges and anemones on the walls of the arch.

Left A diver illuminates the colourful sponges in Rikoriko Cave

130 m (427 ft)-long, 80 m (262 ft)-wide and 35 m (115 ft) from water to the roof, the entry between two pinnacles is full of fish action due to the current but this can be fierce. At the arch itself, divers feel that they are swimming through a cathedral.

The depth close to the arch is no more than 20 m (66 ft) and there are several fish species. Inside the arch divers find Lord Howe butterflyfish, kingfish (amberjack), porae, golden snapper and it is common to encounter shoals of dozens of stingrays. Outside the arch there are anemones, triplefins, blennies, soft corals and small caverns with lots of colourful sponges.

FACTS

CLIMATE
Subtropical with temperatures averaging 20°C (68°F) all year round. Cool, wet and windy in winter (June-October), often very dry from January to March.

SEASONALITY
Year round but the water is warmer from December to May.

GETTING THERE
Fly to Auckland then either fly to Whangarei or by road to Tutukaka. A number of charter boats operate from Tutukaka, which is 30 km (19 miles) from Whangarei.

WATER TEMPERATURE
14°C (57°F) in winter, 23°C (73°F) in summer. Warmest from January to May.

QUALITY OF MARINE LIFE
Very diverse with microclimates from both cold and warmer water. Fish life includes eagle rays and stingrays, moray eels and reef fish. Kelp and encrusting species are also found.

DEPTH OF DIVES
10–50 m (33–164 ft).

SAFETY
Currents on some sites are strong and can be fierce.

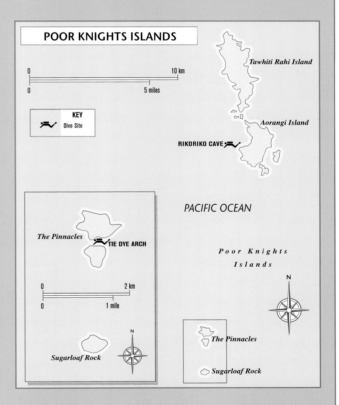

POOR KNIGHTS ISLANDS

0 ———————————— 10 km
0 ———————— 5 miles

KEY
Dive Site

Tawhiti Rahi Island

Aorangi Island

RIKORIKO CAVE

PACIFIC OCEAN

The Pinnacles

TIE DYE ARCH

Poor Knights Islands

0 ———————— 2 km
0 ———— 1 mile

N

The Pinnacles

Sugarloaf Rock

N

Sugarloaf Rock

CAVE DIVING, NEW ZEALAND

INDEX

INDEX

PHOTOGRAPHY CREDITS

1 © Reinhard Dirscherl/SeaPics.com

2 © Doug Perrine/SeaPics.com

5 © Amar & Isabelle Guillen/SeaPics.com

8 © Bob Halstead

10 © Masa Ushioda/SeaPics.com

13 © Masa Ushioda/SeaPics.com

14 © Amar & Isabelle Guillen/SeaPics.com

16 © Doug Perrine/SeaPics.com

19 © Lawson Wood

20 © Lawson Wood

23 © Amos Nachoum/SeaPics.com

24 © James D. Watt/SeaPics.com

25 © C & M Fallows/SeaPics.com

29 © Lawson Wood

30 © Lawson Wood

33 © Lawson Wood

34 © Lawson Wood

36 © Doug Perrine/SeaPics.com

39 © Masa Ushioda/SeaPics.com

40 © Masa Ushioda/SeaPics.com

42 © Masa Ushioda/SeaPics.com

45 © Tanya Burnett/SeaPics.com

46 © Doug Perrine/SeaPics.com

49 © Jack Jackson

50 © Jack Jackson

53 © Lawson Wood

54 © Lawson Wood

56 © Lawson Wood

58 © Robert Yin/SeaPics.com

61 © Jack Jackson

62 © Jack Jackson

64 © Jack Jackson

66 © Lawson Wood

69 © Jack Jackson

70 © Jack Jackson

73 © Lawson Wood

74 © Lawson Wood

77 © Jack Jackson

78 © Jack Jackson

80 A & C Mahaney/ SeaPics.com

82 © Tanya Burnett/SeaPics.com

84 © A & A Ferrari/SeaPics.com

87 © Jack Jackson

89 © Jack Jackson

90 © Jack Jackson

93 © Jack Jackson

94 © Doug Perrine/SeaPics.com

96 © Jack Jackson

99 © Doug Perrine/SeaPics.com

100 © Doug Perrine/SeaPics.com

103 © Mike Veitch/SeaPics.com

104 © Mike Veitch/SeaPics.com

106 © Mike Veitch/SeaPics.com

109 © SeaPics

110 © Doc White/SeaPics.com

112 © Bob Halstead

115 © Lawson Wood

116 © Lawson Wood

118 © Jack Jackson

121 © Jack Jackson

122 © Jack Jackson

125 © Jack Jackson

126 © James D. Watt/SeaPics.com

128 © Jack Jackson

131 © Jack Jackson

132 © Jack Jackson

134 © Jack Jackson

137 © Jack Jackson

138 © Jack Jackson

141 © Mark Strickland/SeaPics.com

142 © Mark Strickland/SeaPics.com

145 © Lawson Wood

146 © Lawson Wood

149 © Tim Rock/SeaPics.com

150 © SeaPics

152 © Andre/SeaPics.com

155 © Manfred Bail/SeaPics.com

156 © Tim Rock/SeaPics.com

159 © Mike Veitch/SeaPics.com

160 © Danja Köhler

162 © Jeff Jaskolski/SeaPics.com

165 © Bob Halstead

166 © James D. Watt/Seapics.com

168 © Bob Halstead

171 © Bob Halstead

172 © Bob Halstead

175 © Phillip Colla/Oceanlight

176 © Phillip Colla/Oceanlight

178 © SeaPics

181 © David B. Fleetham/SeaPics.com

182 © Ofer Ketter/SeaPics.com

185 © Andy Belcher

187 © Andy Belcher

First published in 2009 by New Holland Publishers (UK) Ltd
London · Cape Town · Sydney · Auckland

www.newhollandpublishers.com

Garfield House, 86–88 Edgware Road, London W2 2EA, UK
80 McKenzie Street, Cape Town 8001, South Africa
Unit 1, 66 Gibbes Street, Chatswood, New South Wales, Australia 2067
218 Lake Road, Northcote, Auckland, New Zealand

10 9 8 7 6 5 4 3 2 1

192

ISBN 978 1 84773 541 6

Commissioning Editor: Ross Hilton
Design: Roland Codd
Cartography: Stephen Dew
Production: Marion Storz
Editorial Direction: Rosemary Wilkinson

Reproduction by Pica Digital Pte Ltd, Singapore
Printed and bound in Tien Wah Press (Pte) Ltd, Singapore

Disclaimer

The maps in this book are for illustration purposes only and should not be used for navigation.